Student Study Guide

to accompany

Exceptional Children
An Introduction to Special Education

Seventh Edition

William L. Heward
The Ohio State University

Prepared by

Sheila R. Alber
University of Southern Mississippi

David F. Bicard
Florida International University

Merrill
Prentice Hall

Upper Saddle River, New Jersey
Columbus, Ohio

10 9 8 7 6 5 4 3 2 1

ISBN: 0-13-048734-1

TABLE OF CONTENTS

Introduction

TO THE STUDENT

We have prepared this Study Guide to the seventh edition of William Heward's textbook *Exceptional Children: An Introduction to Special Education* with you, the student, in mind. This comprehensive review of your textbook's content should provide you with a useful resource for learning about exceptional children, their families, and the field of special education. You will discover that there is a great deal to learn about exceptional children and that mastery of this subject requires diligent study. Our goal is that this Study Guide will contribute to your success in this very important topic—understanding and teaching exceptional children.

USING THIS GUIDE

This Study Guide is divided into chapters corresponding to those in your textbook, and each chapter consists of eight sections: Focus Questions, Essential Concepts, Chapter at a Glance, Guided Review, In Class Activities, Homework, Objectives, and Self-Check Quiz. We have provided suggestions for using the various sections of the Student Study Guide's chapters to assist you in planning and organizing your study routines so that you may attain mastery of your textbook's content.

FOCUS QUESTIONS

Each chapter in your textbook begins with a series of Focus Questions. In the Study Guide, we provide a brief discussion that responds to each question. You will find that the Focus Questions do not necessarily deal with specific details as much as they address larger issues and concepts that have general importance to a category of exceptionality or to the field of special education as a whole. You may find the Focus Questions useful as an introduction to your reading of a chapter or as a review of the chapter's contents.

ESSENTIAL CONCEPTS

The Essential Concepts section provides an overview of the key points for each chapter. It may be helpful to read the essential concepts prior to reading the chapter.

CHAPTER AT A GLANCE

The Chapter at a Glance features are a quick reference to the main topics, key points, and key terms in each of the textbook's chapters. As with the Focus Questions, you may find the Chapter at a Glance useful as a review or an introduction to each chapter.

GUIDED REVIEW

The Guided Review is designed so that you may complete it while you read the chapter. It allows you to actively respond to the information in the textbook, and it focuses your attention on important points and details from the chapter. Additionally, it provides a useful set of notes to study. You may check the accuracy of your responses to the Guided Review by referring to the Companion Website.

IN CLASS ACTIVITIES

The In Class Activities provided in this Study Guide are also included in the Instructor's Manual that accompanies the textbook. For each chapter, the In Class Activities include one or more of the following: small group activities, response card activities, whole class discussion activities, and/or simulations.

HOMEWORK

The homework assignments are also included in the Instructor's Manual. Your instructor may require you to complete one of the 2-3 homework assignments listed for each chapter in your Study Guide. The homework assignments require you to apply your knowledge by writing a position paper discussing a particular issue related to the chapter's content or to design instruction related to the disability category you are studying.

OBJECTIVES

Objectives are provided for each chapter to guide your study of the critical information presented in the chapter. You may read the objectives prior to reading the chapter to focus your study on the most important information.

SELF-CHECK QUIZ

Each chapter also includes a self-check quiz so that you may check your knowledge and comprehension of the content presented in the chapter. An answer key is provided for each of the quizzes at the end of the Study Guide so that you can check the accuracy of your responses.

CHAPTER ONE
DEFINING SPECIAL EDUCATION

Focus Questions_____

- **When is special education needed? How do we know?**

  Determining the need for special education is a complex and controversial task that is influenced largely by one's views of the purposes of special and general education programs. Basically, special education is needed when the physical attributes and/or learning abilities of students differ from the norm-either below or above-to such an extent that an individual educational program is required to meet their needs. How is the need for special education determined? The need is readily apparent for some students-their academic, physical, and/or social deficits or excesses are obvious. With other students, the need is not so obvious. Highly skilled and dedicated general education teachers working with other specialists and concerned parents are needed to identify students' needs and to provide specialized services.

- **If categorical labels do not help a teacher decide what and how to teach, why are they used so frequently?**

  Some educators argue that a system of classifying children with exceptionalities is a prerequisite to providing the special programs these children require. Labeling allows special-interest groups to promote specific programs and spur legislative action, which ultimately makes more visible to the public the needs of exceptional children. In addition, labeling helps professionals communicate with one another, can influence education or treatment, and may lead to a protective response in which children are more accepting of the atypical behavior of the child with disabilities. Other educators propose alternative approaches to classifying exceptional children that focus on educationally relevant variables, like the curriculum and skill areas that they need to learn.

- **Why have court cases and federal legislation been required to ensure that children with disabilities receive an appropriate education?**

  Providing equal educational opportunities and services for children with disabilities closely parallels the struggle by minority groups to gain access to and enjoy the rights to which all Americans are entitled. An awareness of the barriers that have deprived these children of equal educational opportunity is important. Some people believe that special education is too expensive and that many children with exceptionalities cannot benefit from educational programming. Judicial and legislative action has been necessary to establish universal rights for children with disabilities. Our work as special educators is most often performed in local schools, but it is supported and guided by federal and state law.

- **How can a special educator provide all three kinds of intervention-*preventive*, *remedial*, and *compensatory*-on behalf of an individual child?**

  Special educators can and do provide all three types of intervention for children with exceptionalities and their families. Preventive efforts are relatively new, and their effects will not likely be felt for many years. In the meantime, we must count on remedial and compensatory efforts to help people with disabilities achieve fuller and more independent lives.

- **What do you think are the three most important challenges facing special education today? Why? Read your answer again after finishing this book.**

   This question is best answered by reviewing the current challenges presented in this and other chapters in the text. When responding to this question, consider local, state, and national perspectives-for each level of service delivery presents unique challenges. In addition, the attitudes and behavior of people without disabilities toward those with disabilities must be considered when meeting the challenges that face special education today.

Essential Concepts

- Exceptional children differ from normal children to such an extent that an individualized education program is required to meet their educational needs. On one end of the spectrum are children with severe disabilities and on the other are children who demonstrate outstanding academic or artistic achievement. But most importantly, they are our mothers, fathers, brothers, sisters, cousins, aunts, uncles, and maybe even some of the people in this class.

- The four largest categories of exceptional children are learning disabilities, speech and language impairments, mental retardation, and emotional disturbance. The vast majority of children receiving special education have mild disabilities and approximately 75% of students with disabilities receive at least part of their education in regular classrooms.

- Special education is an outgrowth of the civil rights movement of the late 60's and early 70's. In a piece of landmark legislation, PL 94-142, the Federal Government established that a free and appropriate education is the right of all students.

- Special education consists of purposeful intervention efforts at three different levels: preventive, remedial, and compensatory. It is individually planned, specialized, intensive, goal-directed instruction. When practiced most effectively and ethically, special education is also characterized by the use of research-based teaching methods and guided by direct and frequent measures of student performance.

- As a potential future educator, do not become overwhelmed by the current challenges facing the field. Special educators do not face these challenges alone; general education, other social and adult service agencies, and society as a whole must help meet these challenges.

Chapter One at a Glance

Main Topics	Key Points	Key Terms
Who are Exceptional Children?	Exceptional children are those whose physical attributes and/or learning abilities differ from the norm (either below or above) to such an extent that they require an individualized program of special education.	exceptional children impairment disability handicap at-risk
	An impairment refers to the loss or reduced function of a body part or organ.	
	A disability exists when an impairment limits the ability to perform certain tasks.	
	Handicap refers to problems encountered when interacting with the environment.	
	At-risk refers to children who have a greater-than-usual chance of developing a disability.	
How Many Exceptional Children are There?	It is impossible to state the precise number of children with disabilities because of different criteria across states used for identification, the effectiveness of preventive services, and the imprecise nature of assessment.	
	Children in special education represent about 9% of the school age population.	
	The four largest categories are learning disabilities, speech and language impairments, mental retardation, and emotional disturbance.	
	Approximately 75% of students with disabilities receive at least part of their education in regular classrooms.	
Why Do We Label and Classify Exceptional Children?	Some believe that disability labels can have a negative effect on the child and others' perception of her and can lead to exclusion; others believe that labeling is a necessary first step to providing needed intervention and that labels are important for comparing and communicating about research findings.	curriculum-based assessment
	Children can be classified according to the curriculum and skill areas they need to learn. In curriculum-based assessment, students are assessed and classified relative to the degree to which they are learning specific curriculum content.	
Why are Laws Governing the Education of Exceptional Children Necessary?	Children who are different have had a history of being denied full and fair access to educational opportunities.	
	Special education was strongly influenced by social developments and court decisions in the 1950s and 1960s.	

Chapter One at a Glance

Main Topics	Key Points	Key Terms
The Individuals with Disabilities Education Act	The Individuals with Disabilities Education Act encompasses six major principles: zero reject; nondiscriminatory identification and evaluation; a right to a free, appropriate education; education in the least restrictive environment; due process safeguards; and parent and student participation and shared decision making.	zero reject least restrictive environment IEP due process IFSP related services assistive technology manifestation determination
	Special Education law has also extended special education services to infants, toddlers, and preschoolers.	
	The Gifted and Talented Children's Education Act of 1978 provides financial incentives for state and local education agencies to develop programs for students who are gifted.	
	Section 504 of the Rehabilitation Act of 1973 forbids discrimination in all federally funded programs, including educational and vocational programs, on the basis of disability.	
	The Americans with Disabilities Act extends civil rights protection of persons with disabilities to private sector employment, all public services, public accommodations, transportation, and telecommunications.	
What is Special Education?	Special education consists of purposeful intervention efforts at three different levels: preventive, remedial, and compensatory.	preventive primary prevention secondary prevention tertiary prevention remedial rehabilitation compensatory
	Special education is individually planned, specialized, intensive, goal-directed instruction.	
	When practiced most effectively and ethically, special education is also characterized by the use of research-based teaching methods and guided by direct and frequent measures of student performance.	
Current Issues and Future Trends	There exists a gap between what research has discovered about teaching and learning and what is practiced in many classrooms.	
	The recent growth in providing special education and family-focused services for infants, toddlers, and preschoolers who have disabilities or are at risk for developmental delay is a positive sign. Increased efforts must be made to make these services more widely available.	
	Other current issues and future trends are to improve students' transition from school to adult life, and to improve the special education-general education partnership.	

Guided Review _____

I. Who are Exceptional Children?
   - Exceptional children differ from the norm (either below or above) to such an extent that they

     require _____

   - The term "exceptional children" refers to _____

     _____

   - Impairment refers to _____

   - Disability exists when an impairment limits the ability to _____

   - Handicap refers to a problem encountered when interacting with _____

   - "At risk" refers to children who have a _____

II. How Many Exceptional Children are There?
   - It is impossible to state the precise number because _____

     _____

     _____

   - Children in special education represent about 9% of the school age population.

   - The four largest categories are _____

     _____

   - Approximately 75% of students with disabilities receive at least part of their education in _____

     _____

III. Why Do We Label and Classify Exceptional Children?
   A. Possible Benefits of Labeling
      - recognizes differences in learning and behavior, first step to _____

      - may lead to a _____

      - helps professionals _____

      - funding and resources are based _____
      - helps advocacy groups
      - makes special needs more visible

   B. Possible Disadvantages of Labeling
      - focuses on what students _____

      - may stigmatize the student _____

      - may negatively affect _____

- lowers _____

- there is a disproportionate number of _____

- may take the role of _____

- takes away from the child's _____
- suggests that there is something wrong with the child.

- labels tend to have _____

- can be a basis for keeping children out of the _____

- requires great expenditure that might be better spent on _____

C. Labeling and Eligibility for Special Education
   - If losing one's label also means loss of services, the trade-off is not _____

D. Labeling and Prevention of More Serious Problems
   - Necessary first step in serving students with _____

E. Alternatives to Labeling
   - Children can be classified according to the _____

   - Curriculum-based assessment is _____

   _____

IV. Why are Laws Governing the Education of Exceptional Children Necessary?
   A. An Exclusionary Past
      - Children who are different have often been denied _____

      _____

   B. Separate is Not Equal
      - Special education was strongly influenced by social developments and court decisions in the 1950s and 1960s (e.g., Brown v. Board of Education)

   C. Equal Protection
      - All children are entitled to a _____

V. The Individuals with Disabilities Education Act
   A. Six Major Principles of IDEA

      1. Zero reject: _____

      2. Nondiscriminatory Identification and Evaluation: _____

      _____

      3. Free, Appropriate Education: _____

      4. Least Restrictive Environment: _____

      _____

    5.   Due Process Safeguards: _____

    6.   Parent and Student Participation and Shared Decision Making: _____

        _____

B. Other Provisions of the Law
    1.   Extending Special Education Services to Infants, Toddlers, and Preschoolers: _____

        _____

    2.   Related Services and Assistive Technology
    3.   Federal Funding for Special Education
    4.   Tuition Reimbursement: In cases in which an appropriate education cannot be provided in the

        public schools, _____

C. Legal Challenges Based on IDEA
    1.   Extended School Year: Armstrong v. Kline
    2.   Related Services: Board of Education v. Rowley; Irving v. Tatro
    3.   Disciplining Students with Disabilities: Stuart v. Nappi; Honig v. Doe; manifestation
        determination
    4.   Right to Education: Timothy v. Rochester School District

D. Related Legislation
    1.   Gifted and Talented Children
       •   The Gifted and Talented Children's Education Act of 1978 provides financial incentives

       for _____

       _____

    2.   Section 504 of the Rehabilitation Act of 1973

       •   Extends civil rights to _____

    3.   Americans with Disabilities Act
       •   Extends civil rights protection of persons with disabilities to _____

       _____

VI. What is Special Education?
    •   Preventive Intervention: _____

    •   Remedial Intervention: _____

    •   Compensatory Intervention: _____

A. Special Education as Instruction

- Who: _____

- What: _____

- How: _____

- Where: _____

B. Defining Features of Special Education
- Special education is individually _____

_____

VII. Current Issues and Future Challenges
   A. Bridging the Research-to-Practice Gap
   B. Increasing the Availability and Intensity of _____

   C. Improving Students' Transition from _____

   D. Improving the _____

In Class Activities

Small Group Activity: When Does a Disability Become a Handicap?

A disability limits the ability to perform certain tasks (e.g., to see, to read, to walk). A handicap refers to a problem a person with a disability encounters when interacting with the environment. For example, a child with an artificial limb may be handicapped when competing with nondisabled peers in a basketball game, but not handicapped when competing academically in the classroom. With your group, generate a list of 10 types of disabilities. For each disability, describe the circumstances of the environment under which the disability might become a handicap, as well as the circumstances under which the disability would not be a handicap.

Small Group Activity: Discuss Your Experiences with People with Disabilities

In your small group, discuss the following questions related to your experiences with people with disabilities. What experiences have you had with individuals with disabilities in your life? What type of emotional responses have you had when you have seen individuals with disabilities? What preconceived notions have you had about people with disabilities in the past? Have a member of the group record notes. This activity will be followed by a whole class discussion. At the end of the small group discussion report to the class the common and unusual experiences for you and your group members.

Response Card Activity: Identify the Principle of IDEA

In the following examples, identify the principle of IDEA that has been violated: Zero Reject, Nondiscriminatory Identification and Assessment, Free Appropriate Public Education and IEP, Least Restrictive Environment, Due Process Safeguards, or Parent Participation

1. Janice's teachers and principal conducted her annual IEP meeting without inviting her parents.

2. Jamie's parents were told that Jamie could not attend his neighborhood school because his disabilities were too severe.

3. Alice was identified as needing special education services based on the results of one IQ test.

4. Tommy's parents were told that they were not allowed to appeal the school's decision about his placement.

5. Richard, a child with mild learning disabilities, was placed in a self-contained special education classroom even though he could have been successful in a regular classroom.

6. Alexandra's IEP team selected goals and objectives that grossly underestimated her abilities.

7. Conchita, whose first language is Spanish, was identified to receive special education services based on assessments administered to her in English.

8. The administrator at Frank's school refused to let his parents see his school records.

9. The Tall Oaks School District does not have a child find system in place, and many children with disabilities living in the community are not receiving the services they need.

10. Ivana was identified for special education services, but an IEP was never developed for her.

11. Jacob's special education teacher developed goals and objectives for his IEP without input from his parents.

12. Viola is a child with hearing impairments. Her parents were told that if they want her to have an interpreter, they will have to pay for it.

13. The Farmdale County School District uses a full inclusion model with no continuum of service options in place. As a result, many students are inappropriately placed in regular classrooms full time.

14. Sally was evaluated for special education without consent from her parents.

15. Kyle, an 18-year-old student with mental retardation, was told he could no longer attend school after his 19th birthday.

Homework

Write a 2 page paper on one of the following topics

1. Read the prologue and postscript and write a 2- page paper outlining your own philosophy of education.

2. The PROFILES & PERSPECTIVES feature, "What's in a Name? The Labels and Language of Special Education," presents an enlightening commentary on the challenge and importance of changing attitudes and values toward individuals with disabilities. Write a paper addressing the following questions: How does the practice of changing labels affect people with and without disabilities? How can the use of labels both help and hinder children with exceptionalities?

3. The number of students receiving special education under the category of learning disabilities has grown dramatically (from 23.8% to 51.2%) over the last 25 years, whereas the percentage of students with mental retardation has decreased by more than half (from 24.9% to 11.5%). What are the possible reasons for this trend?

What Do You Think?
What are the Characteristics of a Good Teacher?

Think about the teachers you had when you were in elementary school and high school. The teachers that immediately come to mind might be your exceptionally good teachers or exceptionally bad teachers. Write a list of characteristics of your good teachers. Examine your list and prioritize in sequential order the most important attributes of effective teachers. Write an explanation for why you believe each characteristic you selected is important.

Resources and Suggestions for Exploration

Effective Teaching Strategies
http://www.teachervision.com/lesson-plans/lesson-2936.html

Habits of Highly Effective Teachers
http://www.asee.org/prism/November/html/ten_habits_of_highly_effective.htm

A Model of Effective Instruction
http://www.successforall.net/resource/research/modeleffect.htm

How Can Teachers Become More Effective and Efficient at Classroom-Based Assessment?
http://www.eduplace.com/rdg/res/litass/effec.html

Objectives

WHO ARE EXCEPTIONAL CHILDREN
1. List the defining characteristics of exceptional children.
2. Define and describe impairment, disability, and handicap.
3. Define and describe children who are at risk for developing disabilities.

HOW MANY EXCEPTIONAL CHILDREN ARE THERE
1. List the reasons why it is difficult to determine the precise number of exceptional children.
2. List the percentage of school age children receiving special education services.
3. List the percentage of exceptional children representing the four largest categories.

WHY DO WE LABEL AND CLASSIFY EXCEPTIONAL CHILDREN
1. List the benefits of labeling.
2. List the disadvantages of labeling.
3. List the alternatives to labeling.

WHY ARE LAWS GOVERNING THE EDUCATION OF EXCEPTIONAL CHILDREN NECESSARY
1. Define and describe the six major principles of IDEA.
2. Describe the legal challenges based on IDEA.
3. Describe the related legislation with regard to exceptional children.

WHAT IS SPECIAL EDUCATION
1. Compare (describe the similarities) and contrast (describe the differences) the different perspectives of special education.
2. List and describe special education as intervention.
3. List and describe special education as instruction.
4. List the defining features of special education.

CURRENT AND FUTURE CHALLENGES
1. Define and describe the four critical areas in the field of special education.

Self-check Quiz

True/False

1. About as many males as females receive special education services.

2. Most agree that special education labeling should be rejected because of its disadvantages.

3. IDEA applies to gifted and talented children.

4. The term "at risk" refers to children with a greater-than-usual chance of developing a disability.

5. Just as there is regular and special education, there are two distinct kinds of children: the "regular," and the "exceptional."

6. All children with disabilities, without exception, have the right to a free, appropriate program of public education in the least restrictive environment.

7. Public Law 94-142, the Education for all Handicapped Children Act, and the Individuals with Disabilities Education Act are all the same law, as reauthorized and amended by Congress over the years.

8. A person with an impairment has a disability, as those terms are used in special education.

9. The term "exceptional children" refers to those whose physical and/or learning abilities are below the norm to such an extent that special education is necessary to fully benefit from education.

10. A student becomes eligible for special education because of identified membership in a given category.

11. Federal funding reimburses states for the majority of expenses related to provision of special education services.

12. As related services, children with disabilities are entitled to things such as special transportation and counseling if needed to access and benefit from special education.

13. P.L. 99-457 mandated early intervention services to infants and toddlers with disabilities and their families.

14. If a private school placement is needed in order to appropriately educate a student, the placement is made at school expense.

15. Most students are receiving special education services under the category of learning disabilities.

Essay Questions

1. Compare and contrast the terms impairment, disability, and handicap.

2. Describe due process safeguards.

CHAPTER TWO
PLANNING AND PROVIDING SPECIAL EDUCATION SERVICES

*Focus Questions*_____

- **Why must the planning and provision of special education be so carefully sequenced and evaluated?**

  The general goal for special education services is to increase the likelihood that students with disabilities will function as independently as possible in normalized settings. Children with disabilities tend to function below grade level and usually take longer to master essential skills. Therefore, it is important that teachers deliver instruction both effectively and efficiently. Target skills must be carefully selected and sequenced so that students may attain mastery. Additionally, skills must be evaluated and monitored daily so that teachers can make timely instructional decisions. If the student is progressing at an appropriate rate, the teacher can assume that the instructional intervention is effective and should continue using the intervention. If the student is not progressing as expected, the teacher can quickly modify instruction to attain the desired outcomes.

- **Why does the effectiveness of special education require collaboration and teaming?**

  An appropriate education for students with disabilities can best be accomplished when both regular and special education teachers and other service providers work together to provide high quality instruction for all children. The educational needs of exceptional children cannot be resolved by any single individual or professional discipline. Children with disabilities deserve the collective and collaborative efforts of all individuals charged with the responsibility of educating them.

- **How should the quality of a student's individualized education program be judged?**

  The individualized education program (IEP) is the centerpiece of the special education process. IDEA requires that an IEP be developed and implemented for every student between the ages of 3 and 21 with a disability. The IEP is a system for spelling out where the child is, where he should be going, how he will get there, how long it will take, and how to tell when he has arrived. The IEP is a measure of accountability for teachers and schools. The effectiveness of a particular educational program will be judged, to some extent, by how well it is able to help children meet the goals and objectives set forth in their IEPs.

- **Is the least restrictive environment always the regular classroom?**

  The general education classroom is the starting point for the IEP team's discussion of placement. Judgments about the restrictiveness of a given setting must always be made in relation to the individual needs of the student. The regular classroom can promote or restrict a child's educational opportunities and skill development depending on the quality of the learning opportunities the child receives. No setting is, in and of itself, restrictive or nonrestrictive. It is the needs of the child and the degree to which a particular setting meets those needs which defines restrictiveness. Restrictiveness is a feature of place. But the physical place in which children receive their education will rarely be the only variable that determines the appropriateness of their educational opportunities.

- **What elements must be in place for special education to be appropriate in inclusive classrooms?**

  Studies have shown that well-planned, carefully conducted inclusion can generally be effective with students of all ages, types, and degrees of disability. In order for an inclusive placement to be successful, collaboration and teaming are crucial. Professionals who are well trained in inclusive practices can work together to solve learning and behavior problems. Inclusive education would probably be appropriate for many children under these circumstances.

Essential Concepts

- This chapter focuses on four general topics: the IEP (Individualized Education Program), the concept of least restrictive environment, teaming and collaboration, and special education reform.

- PL 94-142 requires that every child receiving special education services have a detailed written plan to guide those services and their delivery. This plan, called an individualized education program (IEP), is cooperatively developed by the school and the child's parents. Although an IEP is not legally binding, it is intended to establish a high degree of accountability for meeting the child's needs.

- At the head of PL 94-142 is the concept of appropriateness and the presumption that what constitutes an appropriate education for one student is not necessarily appropriate for another. The issue of appropriateness cannot be decided solely on the basis of where a student receives his or her education. The restrictiveness of a particular setting should be assessed in relation to the needs of the child. An educational environment must support the academic and social behavior of the teacher, the regular education students, and students with disabilities. The teacher's obligation to teach and all students' opportunities to learn should not be dominated or controlled by any one individual or group.

- Both regular and special educators are responsible for ensuring that the needs of exceptional children are met. Effective educational programs must be cooperatively and collaboratively planned and implemented. Individuals considering a career in education can expect to be involved in teaching exceptional children.

- The passage of PL 94-142 brought to an end the wholesale, and often arbitrary, exclusion of children with disabilities from the full range of experiences available in the public schools. These reforms encourage the school to fit the student rather than have the student fit the school, and they are likely to go a long way toward improving the education of all children. The challenge remains, however, as to how to best meet the needs of exceptional children. While there is little disagreement that education is part of the answer, answers to questions about the content and organization of that education will determine the direction and future of special education.

Chapter Two at a Glance

Main Topics	Key Points	Key Terms
The Process of Special Education	IDEA mandates a particular sequence of events that schools must follow in identifying and educating children with disabilities.	prereferral intervention intervention assistance teams evaluation team multidisciplinary team child study team
	Prereferral intervention is an informal, problem-solving process with two primary purposes: to provide immediate instructional and/or behavioral assistance, and to reduce the chances of identifying a child for special education who may not be disabled.	
	Many schools use intervention assistance teams to help classroom teachers devise and implement adaptations.	
	IDEA requires that all children suspected of having a disability receive a nondiscriminatory, multifactored evaluation.	
	If a child is eligible to receive special education services, an individualized educational program must be developed. The IEP team must also determine the least restrictive environment for the student.	
Collaboration and Teaming	Coordination, consultation, and teaming are three modes of collaboration that team members can use.	coordination consultation teaming interdisciplinary teams transdisciplinary teams
	Multidisciplinary teams are composed of professionals from different disciplines who work independently of one another.	
	Interdisciplinary teams are characterized by formal channels of communication between members.	
	Transdisciplinary teams seek to provide services in a uniform and integrated fashion.	
Individualized Education Program	IDEA requires that an IEP be developed and implemented for every student with disabilities between the ages of 3 and 21.	individualized education program IEP team individualized family services plan (IFSP) individualized transition plan
	Individualized family service plans are developed for infants and toddlers from birth to age 3.	
	The IEP team must include the following members: parents, regular education teacher, special education teacher, LEA representative, an individual who can interpret evaluation results, others at the discretion of the parent or school, and the student (age 14 or older must be invited).	
	IEP Components include present levels of educational performance, annual goals and short term objectives, special education and related services, supplementary aids and services, and projected beginning and ending dates. Transition goals must be included when the child reaches age 14.	

Chapter Two at a Glance

Main Topics	Key Points	Key Terms
Least Restrictive Environment	Least restrictive environment means that to the maximum extent appropriate, children with disabilities should be educated with children without disabilities.	least restrictive environment continuum of services resource room residential facility
	LRE is the setting that is closest to a regular school program and that also meets the child's special education needs.	
	The continuum of services is a range of placement and service options to meet the individual needs of students with disabilities.	
	Before considering if instruction and related services will be delivered in any setting other than the regular classroom, the IEP team must discuss if the annual goals and short term objectives can be achieved in the regular classroom.	
	Removal of a child from the regular classroom should take place only when the nature and severity of the disability is such that an appropriate education in that setting cannot be achieved.	
Inclusive Education	Inclusion means educating students with disabilities in regular classrooms.	inclusion
	Studies have shown that well-planned, carefully conducted inclusion can generally be effective with students of all ages, types, and degrees of disability.	
	A few special educators believe that the LRE principle should give way to full inclusion, in which all students with disabilities are placed full time in regular classrooms.	
	Most special educators and professional organizations, such as CEC, support inclusion as a goal but believe that the continuum of services and program options must be maintained and that placement decisions must be based on the student's individual education needs.	
Where Does Special Education Go From Here?	The promise of a free, appropriate public education for all children with disabilities is an ambitious one, but substantial progress has been made toward fulfillment of that promise.	
	Implementation of IDEA has brought problems of funding, inadequate teacher training, and opposition by some to inclusion of children with disabilities in regular classrooms.	
	Regardless of where services are delivered, the most crucial variable is the quality of instruction that each child receives.	

Guided Review _____

I. The Process of Special Education
    A. Prereferral Intervention
        • Prereferral intervention is an informal, problem-solving process with two primary purposes:

        _____

        _____

        • Many schools use intervention assistance teams to help classroom teachers devise and

        implement _____

    B. Evaluation and Identification
        • IDEA requires that all children suspected of having a disability receive a _____

        _____ evaluation.
        • Technically sound instruments must be used.

        • Tests must not discriminate on the basis of _____

        • Tests must be in the child's native _____

        • Standardized tests must have been validated for _____

        • Standardized tests must be administered by _____

        • The child is assessed in all areas related to the suspected disability by a _____

        _____

    C. Program Planning
        • If a child is eligible to receive special education services, an _____

        _____ must be developed.

    D. Placement
        • The IEP team must also determine the _____

    E. Review and Evaluation
        • The IEP must be thoroughly and formally reviewed on an _____ basis.

        • The IEP document has limited usefulness without _____

        _____

II. Collaboration and Teaming
    A. Collaboration
        • Coordination requires only ongoing communication and cooperation to ensure that services

        are provided in a _____

        • In consultation, team members provide _____

B. Teaming
- Multidisciplinary teams are composed of professionals from different disciplines who work

  _____ of one another.

- Interdisciplinary teams are characterized by _____

  _____

- Transdisciplinary teams seek to provide services in a _____

III. Individualized Education Program
- IDEA requires that an IEP be developed and implemented for every student with disabilities

  between the ages of _____

- Individualized family service plans are developed for _____

A. IEP Team
- The IEP team must include the following members: _____

  _____

  _____

B. IEP Components
- A statement of _____ of educational performance

- A statement of _____ and short term objectives

- A statement of special education and related services, and _____

- An explanation of the extent to which the student will _____

  _____

- Individual modifications

- The projected date for the _____ of services

- A statement of how the child will be assessed

- Beginning at age 14, a statement of _____

- Beginning at age 16, an _____

C. IEP Functions and Formats
- IEP formats vary widely across school districts, and schools may _____

  _____

D. Problems and Potential Solutions
   - Properly including all of the mandated components in an IEP is no guarantee that the

     document will _____

   - Special and regular educators are working together to create procedures for developing IEPs

     that go beyond compliance with the law and _____

IV. Least Restrictive Environment
   - Least restrictive environment means that to the maximum extent appropriate, children with

     disabilities should be educated with _____

   - LRE is the setting that is closest to a _____

     _____

   A. A Continuum of Services
      - The continuum of services is a range of _____

        _____

   B. Determining the LRE
      - Before considering that instruction and related services will be delivered in any setting other
        than the regular classroom, the IEP team must discuss if the annual goals and short term

        objectives can be achieved in the _____

        Removal of a child from the regular classroom should take place only when _____

        _____

        _____

      - Placement must not be regarded as _____

V. Inclusive Education
   - Inclusion means educating students with disabilities in _____

   - Studies have shown that well-planned, carefully conducted inclusion can be _____

     _____

   - A few special educators believe that the LRE principle should give way to full inclusion, in which

     all students with disabilities are placed _____

   A. Arguments For and Against Full Inclusion

      - Legitimates _____

      - Confuses segregation and integration with _____

      - Is based on a _____

- Supports the primacy of professional decision making

- Sanctions _____

- Implies that people must _____

- Directs attention to _____ rather than to the services and supports people need

- Most special educators are **not** in favor of eliminating the LRE concept and _____

  _____

VI. Where Does Special Education Go From Here?
- The promise of a free, appropriate public education for all children with disabilities is an

  ambitious one, but _____

- Implementation of IDEA has brought problems of _____

  _____

- Regardless of where services are delivered, the most crucial variable is the _____

  _____

In Class Activities

Small Group Activity: Writing Instructional Objectives

Short-term instructional objectives consist of the antecedent conditions for performing a skill, an observable behavior, and criteria for mastery. Use the following guidelines when examining and writing instructional objectives:

1. State the *conditions* (e.g., when presented with: a list of 50 sight words, 10 multiplication problems, 5 paper cut-outs of shapes, a ruler and 5 items to measure, a paragraph written at the third grade level).

2. State what the child will do in *observable* terms (read aloud, solve, answer, point to, identify, spell, compute, recite, state, edit). Do not use terms such as "understand," "appreciate," "know how to," "learn," or "increase knowledge," as these behaviors are not directly observable.

3. State the *criteria* or level of mastery (e.g., 90% accuracy). The criteria set for each objective will depend upon the student's ability level, the difficulty of the task, and the proficiency demanded by the child's natural environment (e.g., you would probably want the child to be able to safely cross the street to 100% accuracy).

Examine the following objectives, identify the missing components, and rewrite them correctly:

1. David will read at a rate of 120 words per minute.

2. Marsha will write the answers to 20 multiplication problems.

3. Sammy will gain an understanding of the Bill of Rights.

4. When presented with pictures of farm animals, Daniel will identify them.

5. Salena will alphabetize words at 85% accuracy.

6. Luther will learn the capitals of the southeastern states.

7. Donald will answer literal comprehension questions to 90% accuracy.

8. When presented with a passage containing mechanical errors, Ella will find and correct each of the errors.

Select one of the following goals, and create 5 instructional objectives related to reaching that goal. The student will:

•   read and comprehend text written at the fifth grade level.

•   solve addition and subtraction problems up to 4 digits with or without regrouping.

•   apply the basic concepts of measurement.

•   demonstrate effective written expression skills to the fourth grade level.

•   demonstrate basic computer and word processing skills.

•   state and follow safety rules for home and school.

•demonstrate organization skills.

Small Group Activity: Prereferral Intervention Strategies

Select one of the following students, and examine his or her inappropriate behaviors to determine prereferral intervention strategies. When creating strategies to address the problems, consider how you might change the inappropriate behaviors by changing the antecedent conditions and/or consequences. Additionally, describe the method you will use to assess the effectiveness of your selected intervention.

Douglas, a sixth grader:
- ignores his teacher when she gives him directions to follow.
- leaves his materials that he needs for class at home, on the bus, in the restroom, or on the playground.
- refuses to complete in-class and homework assignments.
- frequently argues with his classmates.

Julie, a third grader:
- throws tantrums when she does not get her way.
- cries when asked to do an assignment.
- verbally abuses peers and adults.
- wanders quietly around the classroom, but disrupts the class when asked to return to her seat.

Response Card Activity: Identify IEP components

Identify the following statements as present levels or performance, annual goals, or short term objectives.

1. Richard will utilize the strategies of conflict management when faced with a difficult social situation.

2. Karen will orally recite the multiplication tables (0-10) within 10 minutes at 80% accuracy.

3. Susan frequently makes substitutions when reading a passage orally.

4. Joe will comprehend reading passages at the fourth grade level.

5. When presented with a list of 50 basic sight words, Kelly will correctly pronounce at least 40.

6. When presented with 20 subtraction problems with 4 digits, Maria will compute them within 15 minutes to 90% accuracy.

7. Michael is able to answer detail questions when reading a passage up to the second grade level.

8. Janice will master basic written expression skills to the third grade level.

9. When presented with a story starter, Zachary will correctly punctuate a paragraph he has written to 85% accuracy.

10. Aaron is able to read 90% of the words on the Dolch sight word list at the first grade level.

11. Michele will demonstrate appropriate conduct in the general education classroom.

12. Gary is able to add up to three digit numbers with regrouping.

13. Esperanza will identify the states to 80% accuracy when presented with a blank map of the United States.

14. Paul is able to identify basic geometric shapes.

15. Arlene will be able to apply the basic concepts of measurement.

16. When presented with a recipe containing 5 steps, Carolyn will be able to accurately perform each step to 100% accuracy.

17. Jonathan will decode words containing consonant blends.

18. When presented with 20 vowel-consonant-vowel-silent e words, Deanna will decode them to 80% accuracy.

19. Shay is able to solve story problems requiring addition or subtraction.

20. Arisha is able to initiate social interactions with peers.

Homework

List and prioritize the information necessary to determine the least restrictive environment for a child with disabilities. Then write a hypothetical case study describing the social, academic, and behavioral characteristics of the specific child. Include information on the child's age, grade, ethnicity, and specific strengths and weaknesses. Additionally, describe the characteristics of the child's school environment (e.g., teacher training in inclusive education, types of supports in place, demographic information on nondisabled peers). Based on the information you provided, select the least restrictive environment for this child, and defend the appropriateness of your decision.

What Do You Think?
To What Extent Should Students with Disabilities be Included in Regular Classrooms?

Write a 3-4 page position-paper discussing your opinion of the extent to which students with disabilities should be educated in regular classrooms. Should students with disabilities be fully included in regular classrooms for the entire school day or should a student's placement be individually determined using the continuum of placement options? Explain the reasons for your opinion.

Issues that may be addressed in this paper include: the advantages and disadvantages of inclusion for students with and without disabilities, labeling issues, separation and stigma issues, and social and educational outcomes for students with disabilities.

Resources and Suggestions for Exploration

O'Neil, J. (1995). Can Inclusion Work? A Conversation with Jim Kauffman and Mara Sapon-Shevin. Educational Leadership Volume 52 Number 4
http://www.ascd.org/readingroom/edlead/9412/oneil.html

Wang, M.C., Reynolds, M. C., & Walberg, H. J. (1995). Serving students at the margins. Educational Leadership Volume 52 Number 4
http://www.ascd.org/readingroom/edlead/9412/wang.html

Shanker, A. (1995). Full Inclusion Is Neither Free Nor Appropriate. Educational Leadership Volume 52 Number 4
http://www.ascd.org/readingroom/edlead/9412/shanker.html

Objectives _____

THE PROCESS OF SPECIAL EDUCATION
1. Define and describe the process of prereferral intervention.
2. Define and describe the process of nondiscriminatory evaluation.

COLLABORATION AND TEAMING
1. Define and provide examples of the different teaming models.

INDIVIDUALIZED EDUCATION PROGRAMS
1. List the members of the IEP team.
2. List the components of an IEP.

LEAST RESTRICTIVE ENVIRONMENT
1. Define LRE.
2. Describe the process of determining the LRE.

INCLUSIVE EDUCATION
1. Discuss the arguments for and against full inclusion.

WHERE DOES SPECIAL EDUCATION GO FROM HERE?
1. Discuss the challenges that special education faces in the future.

Self-check Quiz _____

True/False

1. Required members of an IEP team include the child's parents and the child, if age 14 or older.

2. IEP formats are dictated by law, and schools may not go beyond those requirements in the information they include.

3. IEPs must state how the child's progress toward annual goals will be measured.

4. Prereferral intervention is a required component of IDEA.

5. One argument against inclusion is that even the most knowledgeable and dedicated teachers in regular classrooms have students who fail to respond to the best practices implemented.

6. A multidisciplinary team is composed of professionals from different disciplines who work independently of one another.

7. According to Giangreco and other full inclusion advocates, inclusion is about restructuring education for all students, rather than specifically being about those with disabilities.

8. Teachers commonly refer children for minor learning problems, the majority not qualifying when evaluated for special education.

9. Terrill has an illness that prevents him from attending school; IDEA allows him to receive services at home or in a hospital.

10. Least restrictive environment and inclusion are synonymous terms.

11. Beginning at age 14, a child's IEP must address transition needs.

12. A child's parents are a part of a school-based evaluation team.

13. IDEA states that goals and objectives on an IEP must be developed by the special education teacher.

14. The intent of LRE is to best fit students into programs.

15. Individualized education programs must be formally, thoroughly reviewed every year.

Essay Questions

1. Discuss the importance of collaboration.

2. Discuss the ways in which a student can participate in assessment, the IEP conference, and instruction.

CHAPTER THREE
SPECIAL EDUCATION IN A CULTURALLY DIVERSE SOCIETY

Focus Questions_____

- **What are the effects of the changing diversity in the population on students and schools throughout the United States?**

The increasing cultural and linguistic diversity of the United States brings to the classroom a rich heritage that can enhance the educational experience for all students. Teachers are challenged to create a culturally responsive curriculum and pedagogy within the classroom. If diverse students are not positively oriented toward both their own culture and the dominant culture, they can become marginalized and their chances of school success can be jeopardized.

- **Why are culturally and linguistically diverse students disproportionately represented in special education?**

The achievement of culturally diverse learners is similar to that of white students in the early grades but falls further behind the longer the students stay in school. For this reason, we must be concerned about the role our education system may be playing in limiting the achievement of students from different cultural groups. Three factors discussed in this chapter that may account for the disproportionate placement of culturally diverse students in special education are: (1) incongruity in interactions between teachers and culturally diverse students and their families, (2) inaccuracy of the assessment and referral process, and (3) ineffective curriculum and instructional practices implemented for culturally diverse students.

- **What initial steps can a teacher take to become a culturally proficient educator?**

While some would suggest that good teachers are born, not made, there are many skills required of classroom professionals that are acquired through experience over time. Culturally responsive assessment, curriculum, and instructional procedures will not become realities until teachers learn to appreciate diversity. The first step in becoming culturally responsive is to develop a general self-awareness and appreciation of diversity. This process begins with a thorough understanding and an appreciation of one's own culture but must then be extended to an understanding, appreciation, and respect of the culture of others.

- **What assessment, curriculum, and instructional methods are effective for students with disabilities from culturally or linguistically different backgrounds?**

Stereotyping and discriminatory practices not only affect assessment results and instructional practices but also influence why a child is initially referred for special education services. Assessment protocols, curriculum decisions, and instructional practices that are not sensitive to the cultural and linguistic diversity present in a classroom can have a negative and lasting impact on children. Formal assessment instruments and curricular materials that have been developed for predominantly Caucasian, middle-class students are likely to give inaccurate results and require unrealistic experiential knowledge for children from culturally and linguistically diverse backgrounds. As with any culture, the family plays a central role in the initial teaching and socialization of children. Educators must be sensitive to the needs of parents and family members from culturally and linguistically diverse backgrounds in planning individualized programs of instruction. Finally, while it would be a mistake to overgeneralize learning styles of particular cultural groups, knowledge about how different groups may respond to traditional teaching-learning situations will assist teachers' decision making and instructional design.

- **If a second-language learner is learning to speak, read, and write English to progress in the school curriculum, does it make any difference whether the limited English proficiency is caused by cultural differences or by a disability?**

  Children with disabilities will experience difficulty learning in their native or dominant language as well as in English. In answering this question, consider whether the child is having difficulty only learning in English or whether the child has difficulty learning regardless of the language used. The teaching methods used in either case may be essentially the same, but the intent and philosophical basis of instruction will be different. Bilingual education is aimed at maximizing nondisabled children's academic development. Bilingual special education is aimed at maximizing exceptional children's achievement. This is a subtle but significant difference in educational focus.

Essential Concepts

- Students from culturally and linguistically diverse background are both underrepresented (gifted and talented programs) and overrepresented (most of the disability categories) in special education.

- Acknowledging, understanding, and respecting cultural diversity are essential attributes of every teacher. It is equally important to understand the potential impact of being educated in a system that serves a predominantly Caucasian, middle-class culture on children from culturally diverse backgrounds. With these points in mind, two issues are particularly pertinent in this chapter: (1) Every teacher must be responsive to the individual needs of every student; and (2) fundamental principles of learning and effective instruction are applicable to all children. In other words, good teaching practices will benefit all student, whatever their cultural background.

- There is often a fine line between understanding and stereotypically assigning common characteristics to every member of a particular group. Just as all children with learning disabilities, mental retardation, or hearing impairments are not the same, educators must not make the mistake of assuming that every member of a given cultural group shares the same attributes. All cultural groups are heterogeneous.

- Three factors may account for the overrepresentation of culturally and linguistically diverse students in many disability categories: (1) incongruity in interactions between teachers and culturally diverse students and families, (2) inaccuracy of the assessment and referral process, (3) ineffective curriculum and instruction.

- Discriminatory practices have occurred and do occur in the assessment of children from culturally diverse backgrounds even though PL 94-142 requires non-discriminatory identification and evaluation. Most educational testes have been standardized on Caucasian, English-speaking, middle-class students, and even tests translated into a child's native language may be inappropriate for children from culturally and linguistically diverse backgrounds. A more meaningful method of assessment of academic and social behavior is to directly observe children not only in school settings but in their neighborhood and family settings as well.

- Respecting the cultural heritage of all students is an important factor to include when designing educational programs to meet the needs of exceptional students. All children bring a social, academic, and cultural background to class with them, and these backgrounds are part of the environment in which learning takes place.

Chapter Three at a Glance

Main Topics	Key Points	Key Terms
Challenges for Education	Although cultural diversity is a strength in our society, many students with disabilities still experience discrimination because of cultural, social class, or other differences from the majority.	demographics
	Culturally diverse learners comprise about 30% of the nation's population.	
	Overall, culturally and linguistically diverse students are more likely to experience challenges and barriers in school achievement, especially if those students also experience poverty.	
	Culturally and linguistically diverse students drop out of school at a much higher rate than white students do; and they are both underrepresented in gifted programs and overrepresented in special education.	
Why are There Disproportionate Placements of Culturally Diverse Students in Special Education?	Three factors may account for the disproportionate placements of culturally diverse students in special education: 1) incongruity between teachers and culturally diverse learners, 2) inaccurate assessment and referral, and 3) ineffective curriculum and instruction.	culture microcultures
	Cultural heritage is learned. Culture is shared. Culture is an adaptation. Culture is a dynamic system that changes constantly.	
	The likelihood of obtaining valid, accurate, and unbiased assessment results is lower when the student is from a culturally different background.	
	Learning deficits result from the constraints that chronic poverty or unaddressed trauma can place on children's access to the experiences and knowledge deemed normative for all children by the cultural groups with which their families affiliate.	
	Educators who do not adapt the curriculum for diversity in schools today will most likely perpetuate the disproportionate referral of culturally diverse students into special education.	
Becoming a Culturally Proficient Educator	Cultural self-awareness is the bridge to learning about other cultures.	minority culturally diverse
	The term "minority" represents an attempt to categorize by race, not by culture. The majority of students now enrolled in the 25 largest school districts in the U.S. are from ethnically diverse "minority" groups.	
	The term culturally diverse implies no judgment of a culture's value and does not equate cultural diversity with disability.	

Chapter Three at a Glance

Main Topics	Key Points	Key Terms
Becoming a Culturally Proficient Educator (continued)	Practitioners must understand that parents are "life educated" and know their children better than anyone else.	
	Barriers that might exist in working with parents and families from diverse backgrounds include: language skills, home/school partnerships, work interference, knowledge of the school system, self-confidence, and past experiences.	
	To overcome these barriers, teachers should have a general understanding of the culture, child rearing practices, family patterns, views of exceptionality, availability and use of community resources, linguistic difference, acknowledging own biases, beliefs about professionals, nonverbal communication styles, view of medical practices, sex roles, and religion.	
Appropriate Assessment of Culturally Diverse Students	Assessment of students for placement in special education should be fair; referral should be based on each child's needs.	alternative assessment portfolios
	Alternative assessment models integrate a variety of measures such as direct observations, portfolios, self-reports, inventories, and interviews.	
	Alternative assessment allows for exploration of numerous factors and confounding variables (e.g., environmental deprivation, poverty, health problems, language and cultural differences).	
	IDEA specifies that assessment for the purpose of identification and placement must be conducted in the child's native language, however, few reliable tests are available in languages other than English.	
Culturally Responsive Curriculum and Instruction	A culturally responsive pedagogy includes the following: context-embedded instruction, content-rich curriculum, equitable pedagogy, interactive and experiential teaching, and classroom materials and school environment.	context-embedded instruction content-rich curriculum equitable pedagogy transitional approach maintenance approach restoration approach enrichment programs
	Four approaches to bilingual education include the transitional approach, maintenance approach, restoration approach, and enrichment programs.	
Thinking About Your Own Practice	Six promising practices to reduce disproportional representation in special education are: special education reform, prereferral intervention, training, recruiting and retaining, family involvement, and alternative assessment strategies.	
	Regardless of cultural background, all children benefit from good, systematic instruction. The teacher must be sensitive to the effects of cultural and language differences on a child's responsiveness to instruction.	

Guided Review

I. Challenges for Education
    A. Changing Demographics
        • African American, Latino, Asian American, and American Indian comprise _____ of the nation's population
        • "Minority" groups are expected to comprise more than _____ of the population by 2020, and _____ by 2040.
        • Poverty
        • Overall, culturally and linguistically diverse students are more likely to experience _____

        _____

    B. School Dropout
        • Culturally and linguistically diverse students drop out of school at a much higher rate than

        _____

    C. Disproportional Representation in Special Education
        • Culturally and linguistically diverse students are both _____ and

        _____ in special education.

II. Why are There Disproportionate Placements of Culturally Diverse Students in Special Education
    A. Incongruity between Teachers and Culturally Diverse Learners
        • Without a solid understanding of how culture influences both students and school personnel,

        _____

        • Definition of culture: _____

        _____

        • Four basic characteristics of culture: _____

        _____

        • There is heterogeneity within cultures.

    B. Inaccurate Assessment and Referral
        • The likelihood of obtaining valid, accurate, and unbiased assessment results is lower when the

        student is _____

        • Learning deficits result from the constraints that chronic poverty or unaddressed trauma can

        place on children's access to _____

        _____

    C. Ineffective Curriculum and Instruction
        • Educators who do not adapt the curriculum for diversity in schools today will most likely

        _____

III. Becoming a Culturally Proficient Educator
- Six phases on the continuum of teacher awareness and actions: _____

_____

A. Teacher Awareness and Development
- Cultural self-awareness is the bridge _____
1. Understanding Verbal and Nonverbal Communication Styles
- Teacher-student and teacher-parent communication may be enhanced by some

  knowledge of the different significance attached to _____

  _____

2. Understanding Multicultural Terminology
- The term "minority" represents an attempt to categorize by _____
- The majority of students now enrolled in the 25 largest school districts in the U.S. are

  from _____

- The term culturally diverse implies no judgment of a culture's _____ and does

  not equate cultural diversity with _____

B. Working with Culturally and Linguistically Diverse Families
- Many families may be English-language learners, be less well educated, have low socioeconomic status, or be undocumented immigrants.

- Practitioners must understand that parents are _____

  _____

- If families are suspected to be undocumented immigrants, they are naturally fearful of

  _____

- Families from culturally diverse backgrounds tend to be _____
- Families may have differing views about disability, and some may hold idiosyncratic

  ideologies and practices about the _____

- The educational system may be extremely _____ to the family
- Barriers that might exist in working with parents and families from diverse backgrounds

  include: _____

  _____

- To overcome these barriers, teachers should have a general understanding of the culture, child rearing practices, family patterns, views of exceptionality, availability and use of community resources, linguistic difference, acknowledging own biases, beliefs about professionals, nonverbal communication styles, view of medical practices, sex roles, and religion.

IV. Appropriate Assessment of Culturally Diverse Students
    A. Varied and Alternative Methods of Assessment
       • Alternative assessment supplements the results of _____

       • Alternative assessment models integrate a variety of measures such as _____

         _____

       • Alternative assessment allows for exploration of the _____

         _____ (e.g., environmental deprivation, poverty, health problems, language, and cultural differences)

    B. Attention to Language
       • IDEA specifies that assessment for the purpose of identification and placement must be

         conducted in the child's _____

       • Few reliable tests are available in _____
       • Language-proficiency tests coupled with an analysis of real or authentic conversational

         factors provide the opportunity to assess _____

    C. Avoiding Discrimination and Bias
       • Assessment and Intervention Model for the Bilingual Exceptional Students

V. Culturally Responsive Curriculum and Instruction
    A. A Culturally Responsive Pedagogy
       • Context-embedded instruction

       • _____

       • _____
       • Interactive and experiential teaching

       • _____

    B. Bilingual Special Education
       • Transitional approach: _____

         _____

       • Maintenance approach: _____

       • Restoration model: _____

       • Enrichment programs: _____

VI. Thinking About Your Own Practice
   • Six promising practices to reduce disproportional representation in special education: _____

   _____

   _____

   • Regardless of cultural background, all children benefit from _____
   • The teacher must be sensitive to the effects of cultural and language differences on a child's responsiveness to instruction.

In Class Activities

Small Group Activity: Cultural Self-awareness

In this cooperative learning group activity, students should get into groups of five. Decide on the following roles for each member of the group: leader, facilitator, recorder, time-monitor, and presenter. The jobs for each person are as follows:
Leader: Guide the discussion and make sure each viewpoint is clarified for the group.
Facilitator: Make sure everyone participates.
Recorder: Write down the main points of the discussion.
Time-monitor: Make sure the group stays on task during the discussion.
Presenter: Present the results of the group to the class after the group activity.

Discuss the following questions with your group and provide personal examples to illustrate your points.

1.   How has your cultural group influenced your attitudes?

2.   How has your cultural group influenced your values?

3.   How has your cultural group influenced your life style decisions?

4.   To what extent did cultures influence the educational practices in your K-12 school experience?

5.   How will the influences of your culture influence your decisions/practices as a classroom teacher?

6.   What educational practices at your college or university have promoted your capacity to teach students from diverse backgrounds? What practices have interfered?

Homework

Re-read the TEACHING & LEARNING segment "Questions Teachers Should Ask About a New Culture or Ethnic Group." Identify a cultural group by country and write a research paper answering the seven questions outlined in the section.

Group Project: Develop a Collaborative Multicultural Unit

Team up with 4 other students in your class to create a multicultural thematic unit.
1.   Select a grade level for which you will be developing the unit.
2.   Select a few instructional objectives for each skill and/or content area your group will be addressing in the unit (e.g., math, language arts, science, social studies, physical education, art, music).
3.   Select a cultural group around which you will be planning the unit.
4.   Each member of the group will select a skill or content area for which he or she will be responsible.
5.   Gather information and materials about the cultural group your team has decided to study, and create 3 to 5 lesson plans for your designated skill/content area. For example, if the team were studying Chinese culture, the person responsible for the math skill area may develop problem-solving lessons using tangrams or magic squares.
6.   Present your multicultural unit to the class.

What Do You Think?
How can we solve the problem of disproportionate placement of students with disabilities in special education?

Students who are members of culturally diverse groups are typically underrepresented in gifted programs and overrepresented in special education programs for students with disabilities. Three factors may account for the disproportionate placement of students in special education: incongruity in interactions between teachers and culturally diverse students and families, inaccuracy of the assessment and referral process for culturally diverse students in special education, and ineffective curriculum and instructional practices for culturally diverse students. Many culturally and linguistically diverse students in special education have difficulties that were "pedagogically induced" and acquired their disability labels because instruction was not adjusted to fit their individual needs or background.

As a teacher, what steps will you take to prevent "pedagogically induced" disability labels of culturally diverse students? When answering this question, examine the following issues: interactions with culturally diverse students and their families, instructional strategies, instructional materials, alternative methods of assessment, managing the instructional environment, and dealing with your own possible inherent biases. Use specific examples to illustrate your points.

<u>Resources and Suggestions for Exploration</u>

Prereferral Activities: One Way to Avoid Biased Testing Procedures and Possible Inappropriate Special Education Placement for American Indian Students
http://www.ncbe.gwu.edu/miscpubs/jeilms/vol15/preferral.htm

The Inclusive Education Movement & Minority Representation in Special Education: Trends, Paradoxes and Dilemmas
http://www.isec2000.org.uk/abstracts/keynotes/artiles.htm

Five Strategies to Reduce Overrepresentation of Culturally and Linguistically Diverse Students in Special Education
http://www.teachervision.com/lesson-plans/lesson-6049.html

Exploring Relationships between Inappropriate and Ineffective Special Education Services for African American Children and Youth and their Overrepresentation in the Juvenile Justice System
http://www.law.harvard.edu/civilrights/conferences/SpecEd/osherpaper2.html

Disproportionality Issues in the Implementation of IDEA '97
http://www.nasponline.org/publications/cq284disproportion.html

Cultural Diversity and Academic Achievement
http://www.ncrel.org/sdrs/areas/issues/educatrs/leadrshp/le0bow.htm

Learning disabilities occurring concomitantly with linguistic differences.
http://www.louisville.edu/library/distance/e-reserve/summer/1998/EDSP640-90/ortiz.html

Objectives

CHALLENGES FOR EDCUATION
1. List the challenges facing educators.

WHY ARE THERE DISPROPORTIONATE PLACEMENTS OF CULTURALLY AND
LINGUISTICALLY DIVERSE STUDENTS IN SPECIAL EDUCATION
1. Define and describe the three identified reasons that may cause children from diverse backgrounds to be
    disproportionally represented in special education.
2. Define culture.

BECOMIMING A CULTUALLY PROFICIENT TEACHER
1. List the barriers that might exist when working with students from culturally diverse backgrounds.
2. List the strategies to overcome the barriers.

APPROPRIATE ASSESSMENT OF CULTURALLY DIVERSE STUDENTS
1. Identify and describe appropriate alternative assessment methods for students from culturally diverse
    backgrounds.

CULTURALLY RESPONSIVE CURRICULUM AND INSTRUCTION
1. Describe the characteristics of a culturally responsive pedagogy.

THINKING ABOUT YOUR OWN PRACTICE
1. Identify the six practices that may help to reduce disproportional representation in special education.

Self-check Quiz

True/False

1.   Culturally competent teachers are "colorblind"; e.g., they would agree that all students should be treated
     alike in order to be fair to all.

2. Incongruity between teachers and culturally diverse students is expected to decrease as the proportion of
    white teachers continues to shrink over the next decade.

3. The primary issue with inaccurate assessment and referral is one of isolating "within the child" factors,
    i.e., disability, from factors dependent upon external contexts such as culture and language.

4. Low student achievement and high drop out rates are inherently a function of the family or the social or
    ethnic background of students.

5. Poverty and single parent families are the two variables most highly correlated with increased risk for
    childhood disability.

6. The process of becoming a culturally proficient teacher begins with gaining knowledge about other
    cultures.

7. Alternative assessments are most appropriate for some culturally and linguistically diverse students.

8. Court decisions and legislation prohibit discrimination of educational opportunity by schools in the areas
    of gender, race, or ability to speak English.

9. Some bilingual programs exist in the U.S. which focus on teaching English-speaking students another language.

10. Blacks have the highest dropout rate of any identified minority group.

11. Most bilingual education programs use a maintenance or transitional approach.

12. The focus in bilingual special education is to individually design an intervention program to learn English.

13. The cultural background and expectations of some children will prevent them from benefiting from good, systematic instruction.

14. The transitional approach in bilingual education programs helps the student function in both the native language and English, promoting bilingualism.

15. Because poverty, belonging to a single-parent family, and cultural background predict disability, referral should be based on a child's background as well as his needs.

Essay Questions

1. Critique the following definition of culture: "It consists of our background and shared history, and determines who we are. Being static, it provides stability in our lives and a homogeneity to our experiences, [and] is therefore is the primary way in which a teacher can understand student achievement."

2. Describe awareness and actions a teacher might go through as he moves from one end of the continuum of cultural proficiency to the other.

CHAPTER FOUR
PARENTS AND FAMILIES

Focus Questions _____

- **What can a teacher learn from the parents and families of students with disabilities?**

  For the vast majority of children, parents are their first teachers; and parents, for the most part, know their children best. It, therefore, would be short-sighted for educators not to develop productive parent-teacher partnerships. What teachers can learn from the parents and families of children with disabilities is as varied as the children themselves. Some parents will have a great deal to offer by providing a deeper understanding of the overall needs of their child, helping identify meaningful instructional objectives, encouraging extra practice of skills at home, and teaching their children new skills themselves. Other parents may be less involved in their child's education but can still provide important insight about the educational needs of their children.

- **How does a child with disabilities affect the family system and roles of parents?**

  Evidence suggests that many parents of children with disabilities experience similar reactions and emotional responses and that most go through an adjustment process as they try to work through their feelings. Parents of a child with disabilities move from shock, denial, and disbelief to anger, guilt, depression, rejection, and overprotectiveness, and eventually to acceptance. However, parents and family members do not always move through the same stages in the same order or at the same time.

- **How can a teacher who is not the parent of a child with a disability communicate effectively and meaningfully with parents of exceptional children?**

  Educators who are not parents of a child with disabilities cannot know the 24-hour reality of being the parent of a child with disabilities or chronic illness. Nonetheless, they should strive for an awareness and understanding of how a child with special needs affects (and is affected by) the family system. This increased awareness of the challenges a family of a child with disabilities faces is the first step to effective and meaningful parent-teacher communication.

- **How might the nature or severity of a child's disability change the objectives of parental and family involvement?**

  Parental involvement in any child's education is important. For parents of exceptional children, this involvement may be even more critical. Nondisabled children acquire many functional skills without a great deal of direct instruction and deliberate practice (e.g., talking, playing, walking). The skills seem to come "naturally" to them. On the other hand, many children with disabilities will not acquire these same skills as easily as their "typical" peers. Their parents, therefore, must know how to directly and systematically teach these skills. The nature or severity of some children's disabilities also requires that parents learn to use special equipment such as hearing aids, braces, wheelchairs, and adapted eating utensils. For many children with disabilities, acquiring and maintaining skills requires considerable practice. Parents and teachers can work together to facilitate additional practice.

- **How much involvement by parents and families is enough?**

  In general, more parent involvement is better for helping the child with disabilities attain their goals. Sometimes, however, the time and energy required for parents to participate in home-based tutoring programs or parent education groups cause stress among family members or guilt if parents cannot fulfill teachers' expectations. The Mirror Model for Parental Involvement recognizes that parents have a great deal to offer, as well as a need to receive services from special educators. All parents should be expected to provide and obtain information. Most parents will be active participants in IEP planning. Fewer parents will participate in or contribute to workshops and extended parent education groups.

Essential Concepts

- Parents and family members are the best advocates and the first teachers for their children. Parents are indispensable partners in the educational process. They want to be involved in their child's education. The family is likely to be the only group of adults involved with a child's educational program throughout his or her entire school career. In addition, research and practice have shown that educational programs are more effective when parents are involved.

- It is important for teachers to recognize that there are many (and sometimes difficult) roles that parents must fulfill. These roles include caregiver, financial provider, teacher, counselor, parent of siblings without a disability, marriage partner, and advocate.

- Effective parent-teacher partnerships are characterized by family members and professionals jointly pursuing shared goals in a climate of mutual respect. Regular two-way communication with parents is the key operational element of an effective parent-teacher partnership.

- Preparation is the key to effective parent-teacher conferences. Preparation for the conference entails establishing specific objectives, obtaining and reviewing the student's grades, selecting examples of the student's work, and preparing for an agenda of the meeting.

- Professionals who work with parents should support families and value family needs. Family-centered services are predicated on the belief that the child is part of the family system and that effective change for the child cannot be achieved without the help of the entire family.

Chapter Four at a Glance

Main Topics	Key Points	Key Terms
Support for Family Involvement	Families have the greatest vested interest in their children and are usually the most knowledgeable about their needs. The family is likely to be the only group of adults involved with a child's educational program throughout his or her entire school career. Today's special educator attaches high priority to designing and implementing instructional programs that enable students with disabilities to use and maintain academic, language, social, self-help, recreation, and other skills in school, at home, and in the community. IDEA requires collaboration between schools and families.	collaboration
Understanding Families of Children with Disabilities	Parents go through a period of adjustment when they find out their child has a disability. Educators should refrain from expecting parents to exhibit any kind of "typical" reaction. The roles of the exceptional parent include: caregiver, provider, teacher, counselor, behavior support specialist, parent of siblings without disabilities, marriage partner, information specialist/trainer for significant others, and advocate. Respite care is the short-term care of a family member with disabilities to provide relief for parents from caretaking duties. Parents and families of children with disabilities face new challenges at each stage of their child's development.	respite care advocate
Establishing Parent-Teacher Partnerships	Effective parent-teacher partnerships are characterized by family members and professionals jointly pursuing shared goals in a climate of mutual respect. Regular two-way communication with parents is the key operational element of an effective parent-teacher partnership. The following are principles of effective communication: accept parents' statements, listen actively, encourage, and stay focused. Differences in the cultural and linguistic beliefs and practices of professionals and families often serve as barriers to parent involvement. Road blocks to communication include: treating parents as vulnerable clients, keeping professional distance, treating parents as if they need counseling, blaming parents for their child's condition, disrespecting parents as less intelligent, treating parents as adversaries, and labeling parents. Dialoguing is an approach to conflict resolution where both parties try to see both points of view.	positive behavioral support cultural reciprocity dialoguing

Chapter Four at a Glance

Main Topics	Key Points	Key Terms
Methods of Home-School Communication	Parent-teacher conferences should be scheduled regularly. In a parent-teacher conference, parents and teachers can exchange information and coordinate their efforts to assist the child with disabilities in school and at home.	happy grams two-way home-school note systems home-school contracts
	Preparation is the key to effective parent-teacher conferences. Preparation for the conference entails establishing specific objectives, obtaining and reviewing the student's grades, selecting examples of the student's work, and preparing an agenda for the meeting.	
	A suggested 4-step sequence for parent-teacher conferences is: build rapport, obtain information, provide information, and summarize and follow up.	
	Frequent written messages can be an excellent way of maintaining home-school communication. Examples of written messages include: happy grams, two-way home-school notebooks, home-school contracts, and class newsletters and websites.	
	Short, positive telephone calls from the teacher reduce parents' fear that calls from school always indicate a problem.	
Other Forms of Parent Involvement	Parents can serve as effective teachers for their children. Guidelines for home-based parent tutoring include the following: keep sessions short, make the experience positive, keep responses to the child consistent, use tutoring to practice and extend skills already learned in school, and keep a record.	Mirror Model
	Parents can also be involved in parent education and support groups, parent to parent groups, and as research partners.	
	The Mirror Model attempts to give parents an equal part in deciding what services they need and what services they might provide.	
Current Issues and Future Trends	Professionals who work with parents should value family needs and support families.	family-centered services strength-based approach
	Family-centered services are predicated on the belief that the child is part of the family system and that effective change for the child cannot be achieved without helping the entire family.	
	A strength-based approach to family supports assumes that all families have strengths they can build on and use to meet their own needs, accomplish their own goals, and promote the well-being of family members.	

Guided Review _____

I.   Support for Parent and Family Involvement

   - Parents want to be _____

   - Research and practice have shown that educational effectiveness is _____

   _____

   - The law requires _____

   A. Parents Advocate for Change
       - Families have the greatest vested interest in their children and are usually the most

   _____

   B. Educators Strive for Greater Effectiveness and Significance
       - Extensive evidence shows that the effectiveness of educational programs for children with

       disabilities is increased when _____

   C. Legislators Mandate Parent and Family Involvement

       - Each reauthorization of IDEA has _____ parent and
         family participation in the education of children with disabilities.

II. Understanding Families of Children with Disabilities
   A. The Impact of a Child with Disabilities on the Family

       - The grief cycle consists of three stages: _____
       - Educators should refrain from expecting parents of children with disabilities to exhibit any kind
         of typical reaction.

   B. The Many Roles of the Exceptional Parent
       1. Caregiver
           - Additional caregiving responsibilities for children with disabilities can cause added
             stress.
           - Respite care can reduce _____
       2. Provider
           - Parenting children with disabilities is often a financial burden.
       3. Teacher
           - Children with disabilities often do not acquire new skills _____

       _____

       4. Counselor
           - Parents of children with disabilities must deal with the _____

       _____

       5. Behavior Support Specialist
           - Children with disabilities often engage in at least one of the four categories of problem

           behavior: _____

- Parents must be skilled in behavioral support techniques to achieve a semblance of

  _____

6. Parent of Siblings without Disabilities
   - Children are deeply affected by having a _____
   - Parents play a key role in determining the nature of the relationship between their children.
7. Marriage Partner
   - Having a child with disabilities can _____
8. Information Specialist/Trainer for Significant Others
   - Parents must try to ensure that other people interact with their child in ways that support

     their child's _____
9. Advocate
   - Parents of children with disabilities must often advocate for effective educational services

     and opportunities for their children in a society that _____
10. Changing Needs as Children Grow
    - Parents and families of children with disabilities face new challenges at each stage of their child's development.

III. Establishing Parent-Teacher Partnerships
   - Effective parent-teacher partnerships are characterized by family members and professionals

     jointly pursuing _____

A. Principles of Effective Communication
   1. Accepting Parents' Statements
      - conveying through verbal and nonverbal means that what parents say is _____
   2. Listening Actively
      - An active listener not only interprets, sorts, and analyses what the speaker says, but

        _____
   3. Question Effectively
      - Educators should use _____ questions when communicating with parents.
   4. Encourage
      - When presenting a concern, precede with a positive statement and follow with a positive statement.
   5. Stay Focused
      - Conversations between parents and teachers should focus on the child's _____

        _____

B. Identifying and Breaking Down Barriers to Parent-Teacher Partnerships
   1. Cultural Differences
      - Educators can increase the involvement of parents by using culturally responsive and respectful strategies.
   2. Professional Roadblocks to Communication

      - Treating parents as _____

      - Keeping professional distance

      - Treating parents as if they need _____

- Blaming parents for _____

- Disrespecting parents as _____

- Treating parents as _____
- Labeling parents

3. Conflict Resolution through Dialoguing
   - Dialoguing is an approach to conflict resolution in which _____

   _____

IV. Methods of Home-School Communication
   A. Parent-Teacher Conferences
      - Parent-teacher conference should be scheduled _____
      1. Preparing for the conference
         - Preparation for the conference entails _____

         _____

         _____

      2. Conducting the conference
         - A suggested 4-step sequence for parent-teacher conferences is:

            _____

            _____

            _____

            _____

   B. Written Messages
      1. Happy Grams: _____

      2. Two-way home-school notebooks : _____

      3. Home-school contracts: _____

         _____

      4. Class newsletters and websites

   C. Telephone calls
      - Short, positive calls from the teacher reduce parents' fear that calls from school always

         _____

V. Other Forms of Parent Involvement
    A. Parents as Teachers
        • Guidelines for home-based parent tutoring include the following: _____

        _____

        _____

    B. Parent Education and Support Groups
        • By examining the results of needs assessment questionnaires, _____

        _____

    C. Parent to Parent Groups
        • Parent-to-parent programs help parents of children with special needs become _____

        _____

    D. Parents as Research Partners
        • Involving parents in research increases social validity of research.
        • Parents may participate in action research by helping brainstorm research questions, collecting performance data on their children, and sharing the _____

        _____

        _____

    E. How Much Parent Involvement?
        • The Mirror Model attempts to give parents an equal part in deciding _____

        _____

VI. Current Issues and Future Trends
    • Professionals who work with parents should support families and value family needs.
    • Family-centered services are predicated on the belief that the child is part of the family system and that effective change for the child cannot be achieved without the help of the entire family.
    • A strength-based approach to family supports assumes that all families have strengths they can build on and use to meet their own needs, accomplish their own goals, and promote the well-being of family members._____

In Class Activities

Small Group Activity: Simulation of a Parent-Teacher Conference

Role play an interactive parent-teacher conference. Prior to the simulation, determine the child's age, disability, and the area(s) of concern (e.g., specific academic or social skills). Additionally, determine the general attitude of the parent (e.g., cooperative, hostile, etc.). Proceed through the following steps as you role play.

1. Build rapport
2. Obtain information
3. Provide information
4. Summarize and follow up

Response Card Activity: Answer the following true-false questions

1. Families are usually the most knowledgeable about the needs of an exceptional child.

2. Educational programs are not enhanced by parent involvement.

3. The original law for special education (IDEA) made no provision for parent involvement.

4. Most parents usually go through the same life stages when they have a child with a disability.

5. Respite care is an important support for families of children with disabilities.

6. Advocate is not one of the roles of a parent of an exceptional child.

7. The needs of an exceptional child change dramatically as he or she matures.

8. Accepting parents' statements is one of the five principles of effective communication.

9. Cultural differences are not one of the barriers to family involvement.

10. Keeping professional distance is an important component to effective communication.

11. Written messages are often a quick and effective way to communicate with parents.

12. Including parents in action research is a good way to ensure the validity of your teaching.

Homework

Write a 2 page position paper on either of the following topics

1. Throughout the country, many parents of children with autism have begun suing school districts for extramural educational services supplied by behavior analysts. What role should parents have in determining curriculum and instruction for their children? Should school districts have to pay for these services?
2. The TEACHING & LEARNING feature, "A Parent-Professional Partnership in Positive Behavioral Support," describes how a parent-professional partnership was used to systematically find meaningful solutions to a student's behavior problems. How can partnerships between parents and professionals be strengthened?

What Do You Think?
What are the greatest challenges for parents of children with disabilities?

The many roles of parents of exceptional children are discussed in Chapter 4. The roles include caregiver, provider, teacher, counselor, behavior management specialist, parent of other siblings, marriage partner, information specialist/trainer for significant others, and advocate for school and community services. Discuss how the roles and challenges facing parents of children with disabilities differ from the roles and challenges of parents with nondisabled children. Discuss the greatest challenges of parents of exceptional children and how those challenges change as the children progress through each developmental stage (from infancy through adulthood).

<u>Resources and Suggestions for Exploration</u>

Boyce, G. C., Miller, B. C. (1994). Single parenting in families of children with disabilities. <u>Marriage & Family Review, 20,</u> 389-411.

Ehrenkrantz, D., Miller, C., Vemberg, D. K., Fox, M. H. (2001). Measuring prevalence of childhood disability: Addressing family needs while augmenting prevention. <u>Journal of Rehabilitation, 67,</u> 48-55.

Krauss, M. W. (1993). Child-related parenting stress: Similarities and differences between mothers and fathers of children with disabilities. <u>American Journal on Mental Retardation, 97,</u> 393-404.

Marci, J., & Hanline, M. F. (1990). Parenting a child with a disability: A longitudinal study of parental stress and adaption. <u>Journal of Early Intervention, 14,</u> 234-48.

Rodriquez, C. M., Murphy, L. E. (1997). Parenting stress and abuse potential in mothers of children with developmental disabilities. <u>Child Maltreatment, 2,</u> 245-252.

Sexton, D. et al. (1992). Measuring stress in families of children with disabilities. <u>Early Education and Development, 3,</u> 60-66.

Smith, T. B., Oliver, M. N. I., Innocenti, M. S. (2001). Parenting stress in families of children with disabilites. <u>American Journal of Orthopsychiatry, 71,</u> 257-262.

Unger, D. G., Jones, C. W., Park, E., Tressell, P. A. (2001). Promoting involvement between low-income single caregivers and early intervention programs. <u>Topics in Early Childhood Special Education, 21,</u> 197-213.

Warfield, M. E. (2001). Employment, parenting, and well-being among mothers of children with disabilities. <u>Mental Retardation, 39,</u> 297-310.

*Objectives*_____

SUPPORT FOR FAMILY INVOLVEMENT
1.   List the reasons why family collaboration is a necessary component of special education.
2.   Discuss the three factors responsible for increased emphasis on parent and family involvement.
3.   Describe the benefits of family involvement for teachers, parents, and the student.

UNDERSTANDING FAMILIES OF CHILDREN WITH DISABILITIES
1.   Describe the impact on the family of an exceptional child.
2.   Describe the nine roles and responsibilities of parents who have exceptional children.
3.   Discuss the importance of respite care for families of children with severe disabilities.

ESTABLISHING PARENT-TEACHER PARTNERSHIPS
1.   Describe the five principles for effective communication between special educators and families.
2.   Describe the barriers to parent/teacher collaboration.

METHODS OF HOME-SCHOOL COMMUNICATION
1.   List and describe the three most common modes of home-school communication.
2.   Discuss the guidelines for working with parents and families of exceptional children.

OTHER TYPES OF PARENT INVOLVEMENT
1.   Describe the importance of parent education and support.
2.   Describe the guidelines for home-based parent tutoring.
3.   Discuss the mirror model of parent involvement.

CURRENT ISSUES AND FUTURE TRENDS
1.   Discuss the philosophical foundation for family-centered services.
2.   Describe the strengths-based approach to family support.

*Self-check Quiz*_____

True/False

1.   A passive listener may attend to the content of what is said but doesn't interpret it in the context of who said it and how he said it.

2.   It is very important that parents be involved in planning and specifying their preferred needs for parent education and support groups.

3.   Parents have been the primary advocacy force for the education of children with disabilities.

4.   If a parent objects to the consideration of a self-contained classroom, and the teacher responds by saying "let me explain to you why that placement is best," a process of dialogue has occurred.

5.   The roles of behavior support specialist, counselor and even teacher are typical ones taken by parents of children with disabilities.

6.   Extensive evidence shows that children benefit more from their education when parents follow suggestions offered by special educators.

7. One positive effect of mandating parent involvement in special education is that parents no longer need to fulfill the role of advocate.

8. The mirror model for parent involvement assumes that not all parents need all that professionals have to offer and that no parent should be expected to provide everything.

9. IDEA 1997 introduced the requirement of parent and family participation in the education of children with disabilities.

10. Respite care refers to the temporary care of an individual with disabilities by non-family members.

11. Research evidence supports the idea that families move past mere acceptance to an appreciation of the positive aspects of family life with a child with a disability.

12. Children with disabilities are more likely to be reported in abuse and neglect cases, relative to children without disabilities.

13. Despite many benefits, one consistent problem with home-school partnerships is that planning tends to become sidetracked toward goals with less educational relevance.

14. Parents prefer teachers to contact them only when a problem arises.

15. Educators should use open-ended questions as much as possible when communicating with parents.

Essay Questions

1. Summarize the four arguments presented by Giangreco et al. (1988) for viewing active family involvement as the cornerstone of educational planning.

2. Describe the basic principles of effective communication, providing an example for each principle cited.

CHAPTER FIVE
EARLY CHILDHOOD SPECIAL EDUCATION

Focus Questions

- **Why is it difficult to measure the impact of early intervention?**

  The main goal of early intervention programs is to lessen the detrimental effects of some present risk factor on a child's later development. Measures of the effectiveness of an early intervention program entail a number of considerations at different points in time. It is difficult to judge the overall effectiveness of early intervention programs. For example, can we know for certain whether an early intervention program was responsible for a child's needing only occasional tutoring rather than a full-time special education placement? Or can we credit or blame early intervention efforts when a child did not require special education until fourth grade rather than first grade? There are many factors that influence the extent to which a treatment is effective. This is particularly true when the goal of the treatment is preventive, as it is with early intervention programs.

- **How can we provide early intervention services for a child whose disability is not yet present?**

  A child who has been identified as being at risk for developing a disability because of environmental or biological factors should receive preventive programming before any evidence of a disability exists. Parents and teachers do not have to wait until a delay in development occurs before they begin to interact with their children in ways that promote learning and development. Similarly, medical professionals do not need to wait and observe health or biological conditions before they can prescribe various precautionary or preventive procedures for the family to follow on behalf of the child. Intervention programs can never be started too early. Every reasonable precautionary and preventive measure that can be taken to ensure that the child does not develop a disability should be pursued.

- **Which do you think are the most important goals of early childhood special education?**

  The goals of early childhood special education are: (a) support families in achieving their own goals; (b) promote child engagement, independence, and mastery; (c) promote development in all important domains; (d) build and support social competence; (e) facilitate the generalized use of skills; (f) prepare and assist children for normalized life experiences with their families, in school, and in their communities; (g) help children and their families make smooth transitions; and (h) prevent or minimize the development of future problems or disabilities. After studying the goals, you should recognize that many are interrelated and all are intended to lead to increased independence and competency of individual children. All of the goals address the child within the context of the family and the community.

- **What are some ways in which early childhood special education differs from special education for school age children with disabilities?**

  Early childhood special education programs are administered by the state agency instead of the local school district. Young children qualify for early intervention services if there is severe developmental delay, a documented risk, or established medical conditions. Young children do not have to be identified under existing disability categories to be eligible for services. Additionally, a multidisciplinary team develops an Individual Family Service Plan which addresses the needs of the family as well as the child.

- **How can a play activity or everyday routine be turned into a specially designed learning opportunity for a preschooler with disabilities?**

   Play provides children with natural, repeated opportunities for learning. Teachers of young children with disabilities can arrange the child's play environment to promote skill mastery across several developmental domains. Teachers must also monitor the child's progress and make adjustments to the environment that will facilitate the successful development of important skills.

Essential Concepts _____

- The first years of life are a critical period for children who are at risk for or have disabilities. Each month the child risks falling further behind typically developing age mates if early intervention services are not provided. Early intervention services consist of educational, nutritional, childcare, and family supports designed to reduce the effects of disabilities or prevent the development of problems later in life for children at risk. Repeated research clearly demonstrates that the sooner professionals and parents intervene with educational programs, the better the outcome for the exceptional child.

- IDEA guarantees a free, appropriate public education to all children. When it was originally passed, this law did not specifically require that preschool-aged children be served. Amendments to the legislation either mandated educational services or provided monetary incentives to provide those services.

- Involving the family in the assessment and treatment of infants and toddlers has become a crucial component of early childhood special education. In fact, IDEA mandates that it is the family who is the recipient of educational services and that an Individualized Family Service Plan (IFSP) must be developed for families of children receiving intervention services.

- Early intervention has begun to shift away from assessment instruments and procedures that are based entirely on developmental milestones and move towards curriculum-based assessment, which links testing, teaching, and new skill acquisition by the child. In other words, children are being assessed in terms of what they need to be able to do rather than how well their behavior corresponds to age-equivalent norms.

- Special education is known for its team approach to program planning. Nowhere is this truer or more important than in early childhood special education. The parents are not only encouraged to take an active role in their child's education; they are often the recipients of services themselves. A child's progress might be quite difficult without parental assistance and insight. The support both provided and needed by parents in early intervention programs is very important, and teachers must be sensitive to an individual parent's limits of involvement.

Chapter Five at a Glance

Main Topics	Key Points	Key Terms
The Importance of Early Intervention	Early intervention consists of educational, nutritional, childcare, and family supports designed to reduce the effects of disabilities or prevent the occurrence of developmental problems later in life for children at risk for such problems. Research has documented that early intervention can provide both intermediate and long-term benefits for young children with disabilities and those at risk for developmental delay. Benefits in early intervention include: gains in physical development, cognitive development, language and speech development, social competence, and self-help skills.	
IDEA and Early Childhood Special Education	P.L. 99-457 included a mandatory preschool component for children with disabilities ages 3-5 and a voluntary incentive grant program for early intervention services for infants and toddlers and their families. States that receive IDEA funds for early intervention must serve all infants and toddlers with developmental delays or established risk conditions. States may also serve infants and toddlers who fall under two types of documented risk, biological and environmental. The individual family service plan addresses the needs of the child and family and is developed by a multidisciplinary team. Preschool children do not have to be identified under existing categories to receive services. Local education agencies may elect to use a variety of service options.	documented risk developmental delay established risk conditions biological risk conditions environmental risk conditions individualized family service plan (IFSP)
Screening, Identification, and Assessment	Assessment in early childhood special education is conducted for at least four different purposes: screening, diagnosis, program planning, and evaluation. Tests that seek to determine if a child is experiencing a developmental delay usually measure performance in 5 major developmental areas: motor development, cognitive development, communication and language development, social and emotional development, and adaptive development. Program planning uses curriculum-based, criterion-referenced assessments to determine a child's current skill level, identify IFSP/IEP objectives, and plan intervention activities. Many early intervention programs are moving away from assessments based entirely on developmental milestones.	screening diagnosis program planning Apgar scale

Chapter Five at a Glance

Main Topics	Key Points	Key Terms
Curriculum and Instruction in Early Childhood Special Education	Curriculum and program goals for early intervention include: supporting families in achieving their own goals; promoting child engagement, independence, and mastery; promoting development in all important domains; building and supporting social competence; facilitating the generalized use of skills; preparing and assisting children for normalized life experiences with their families, in school, and in their communities; helping children and their families make smooth transitions; and preventing or minimizing the development of future problems or disabilities.	Developmentally Appropriate Practice (DAP) embedded learning
	Developmentally appropriate practices provide a foundation or context from which to build individualized programs of support and instruction for children with special needs.	
	IFSP goals and objectives should be evaluated according to the following five quality indicators: functionality, generality, instructional context, measurability, and relation between long-range goals and short-term objectives.	
	Modifications and adaptations to the physical environment, materials, and activities are often sufficient to support successful participation and learning by a child with disabilities.	
	Teachers should look and plan for ways to embed brief, systematic instructional interactions that focus on a child's IEP objectives in the context of naturally occurring activities.	
	Preschool activity schedules should include a balance of child-initiated and planned activities, large- and small-group activities, active and quiet times, and indoor and outdoor activities.	
Service Delivery Alternatives for Early Intervention	IDEA requires that early intervention services be provided in natural environments to the greatest extent possible.	hospital-based programs home-based programs center-based programs
	Service delivery options for early childhood special education include: hospital-based programs, home-based programs, center-based programs, and combined home-center programs.	
Current Issues and Future Trends	The field of early childhood special education will be advanced by research investigating which combinations of program characteristics are most effective for target groups of children and their families and from studies analyzing the cost-benefit of early intervention.	
	Parents are the most important people in an early intervention program. They can act as advocates, participate in educational planning, observe their children's behavior, help set realistic goals, work in the classroom, and teach their children at home.	

Guided Review _____

I. The Importance of Early Intervention
   A. Examining the Effectiveness of Early Intervention
       1. Research has documented that early intervention can provide both intermediate and long-term benefits for young children with disabilities and those at risk for developmental delay.
       2. Congress identified the following outcomes for early intervention in the 1997 amendments to IDEA:
           - to enhance the development of infants and toddlers with disabilities and _____

             _____

           - to reduce the educational costs to our society, by minimizing the need_____

             _____

           - to minimize the likelihood of institutionalization of individuals with disabilities and

             maximize the potential for _____

           - to enhance the capacity of families to _____

             _____

           - to enhance the capacity of state and local agencies to _____

             _____

II. IDEA and Early Childhood Special Education
   - P.L. 99-457 included a mandatory preschool component for children with disabilities ages 3-5 and

     a voluntary incentive grant program for_____

     _____

   A. Early Intervention for Infants and Toddlers
       - States that receive IDEA funds for early intervention must serve all infants and toddlers with

         _____

       - States may also serve infants and toddlers who fall under two types of documented risk,

         _____

       - The IFSP, a plan that addresses the needs of the child and family, is developed by a

         _____

- Unlike the IEP, an IFSP: _____

  _____

  _____

  _____

- The IFSP must be evaluated once a year and reviewed at _____

B. Special Education for Preschoolers
   - Preschool children do not have to be identified under _____ to receive services.
   - Local education agencies may elect to use a variety of _____

III. Screening, Identification, and Assessment
   - Assessment in early childhood special education is conducted for at least four different purposes:

     _____

   - Tests that seek to determine if a child is experiencing a developmental delay usually measure

     performance in 5 major developmental areas: _____

     _____

     _____

IV. Curriculum and Instruction in Early Childhood Special Education
   A. Curriculum and Program Goals

      - Support families in _____

      - Promote child engagement, _____

      - Promote development in _____

      - Build and support _____

      - Facilitate _____

      - Prepare and assist children for normalized life experiences with _____

        _____

      - Help children and their families make smooth _____

      - Prevent or minimize the development of _____

   B. Developmentally Appropriate Practice recommends the following guidelines for early childhood education programs:
      - Activities should be _____

      - Children's interests and progress should be identified _____

- Teachers should arrange the environment to facilitate _____

  _____

- Learning activities and materials should be _____

  _____

- A wide range of ____ _____

- The complexity and challenges of activities should _____

  _____

C. Selecting IFSP/IEP Goals and Objectives
- Goals and objectives should be evaluated according to the following five quality indicators:

  _____

  _____

D. Instructional Adaptations and Modifications
- Modifications and adaptations to the physical environment, materials, and activities are ____

  _____

- Teachers should look and plan for ways to _____

  _____

- Preschool activity schedules should include a balance of _____

  _____

V. Service Delivery Alternatives for Early Intervention
- IDEA requires that early intervention services be provided in _____

  _____

- Service delivery options for early childhood special education include: _____

  _____

VI. Current Issues and Future Trends
- The field of early childhood special education will be advanced by research investigating which combinations of program characteristics are most effective for target groups of children and their

  families and from _____

- Parents are the most important people in an early intervention program. They can act as _____

  _____

  _____

In Class Activity

The TEACHING & LEARNING feature, "Selecting Toys for Young Children with Disabilities," provides guidelines for selecting the most appropriate types of toys for children with disabilities. Bring in a few toy catalogs and form small groups to identify specific toys and/or activities appropriate for preschoolers. Then require each group to generate a list of how each specific toy promotes growth in the following developmental or skill areas: auditory, language, visual, tactile, gross motor, fine motor, social skills, self-esteem, creativity, and thinking. In addition, require the students to identify how the toys could be adapted or modified to accommodate the needs of students with severe disabilities.

Homework

What Do You Think?
Modifying DAP Guidelines for Students with Disabilities

Almost all early childhood educators share a common philosophy that learning environments and teaching practices should be based on what is typically expected of and experienced by children at their developmental stages. This is called Developmentally Appropriate Practice (DAP). Most early childhood special educators view the guidelines for DAP as providing a foundation or context within which to provide early intervention services for children with special needs. However, a curriculum based entirely on DAP may not be sufficient for children with disabilities. Examine the list of guidelines for Developmentally Appropriate Practice in Chapter 5, and write an explanation of the extent to which DAP guidelines can be modified or are appropriate for students with special needs.

Resources and Suggestions for Exploration

Division for Early Childhood: http://cec.sped.org

National Early Childhood Technical Assistance Center: http://www.nectas.unc.edu/

The Preschool Zone-resources for early childhood special education
http://www.mcps.k12.md.us/curriculum/pep/pz.html

For recommended practices while implementing developmentally appropriate practice
http://www.tr.wou.edu/train/cdcec.htm

Objectives _____

THE IMPORTANCE OF EARLY INTERVENTION
1. Define and describe early intervention services for children with or at risk for the development of disabilities.
2. Summarize the findings of early intervention research that has led to legislation mandating early intervention services.
3. List the outcomes for early intervention services identified by congress.

IDEA AND EARLY CHILDHOOD SPECAL EDUCATION
1. List and describe the regulations pertaining to early childhood special education.

SCREENING, IDENTIFICATION, AND ASSESSMENT
1. List and describe the four purposes of assessment and evaluation in early childhood education.
2. Identify examples of screening tools.
3. Identify examples of diagnostic tools.
4. Define and describe curriculum-based measurement.

CURRICULUM AND INSTRUCTION IN EARLY CHILDHOOD SPECIAL EDUCATION
1. List and describe the eight curriculum and program goals in early childhood special education.
2. Define and provide examples of developmentally appropriate practice.
3. Describe why curriculum based entirely on developmentally appropriate practice may not meet the needs of young children with disabilities.
4. List and describe the five quality indicators of IFSP goals and objectives.
5. Identify examples of curricular and instructional modifications.

SERVICE DELIVERY ALTERNATIVES FOR EARLY INTERVENTION
1. List and describe the types of service delivery options available in early childhood special education.

CURRENT ISSUS AND FUTURE TRENDS
1. List the two areas of need pertaining to research in early childhood special education.

Self-check Quiz _____

True/False

1. Of all people needed to make early intervention effective, parents are considered the most important.

2. Children must be classifiable by other IDEA disability categories (e.g., mental retardation, health impaired) in order to receive early intervention services.

3. Early intervention is sometimes provided to prevent the occurrence of learning and developmental problems in children at risk, even though a child may not currently exhibit deficits.

4. "Children learn by modeling" might be the best slogan for the National Lekotek Center.

5. Federal law currently requires that early intervention services be provided for infants and toddlers with disabilities ages birth through 5.

6. Early intervention is often criticized for many reasons, including that the stigmatizing effect of labeling can lead to a self-fulfilling prophecy.

7. Transitions refer to a child and their family moving from one early intervention program or service delivery mode to another.

8. The term "developmentally appropriate practice" refers to procedural safeguards in assessment of young children.

9. There is little consensus among early childhood special educators on quality goals and objectives for young children in need of services.

10. Early childhood special education refers only to services that are classroom-based.

11. One outcome for early intervention is that it reduces educational costs to our society in the long run.

12. Severity of disability and intensity of intervention are the two factors most highly related to outcome effectiveness of early intervention.

13. Examples of skills in the adaptive domain include brushing teeth and dressing.

14. Curriculum-based assessment is an increasingly popular method for screening children.

15. The Milwaukee Project helps support maternal education and early infant stimulation as reducing incidence of mental retardation.

Essay Questions

1. What advice would you offer a parent in selecting toys for their young child with a disability?

2. Contrast IDEA requirements for service provision to children ages 3 to 5 with those for school-age children.

CHAPTER SIX
MENTAL RETARDATION

Focus Questions

- **What is most important in determining a person's level of adaptive functioning: intellectual capability or a supportive environment?**

As you contemplate this question, think about the quality of life of individuals called mentally retarded. Which factor is more likely to determine whether or not an individual has access to and can function in various school, work, and residential settings? Is it how bright he or she is, or how much support he or she receives? Or is it both? For example, Faye, a young adult with mental retardation, is part of a mobile crew cleaning offices in a large downtown office complex. As Faye's teacher and supervisor, you know her to be a capable worker. She cleans, sweeps, dusts, and performs all her other job-related tasks and fluently. The supervisor of her mobile work crew, however, does not believe in providing varied levels of support for his employees, so Faye is not being successful at her job. As Faye's teacher what should you do? Should you try to improve her abilities or find a more supportive environment for employment?

- **What is to be gained by classifying a child with mental retardation by the intensities of supports she needs to access and benefit from education?**

The AAMR's "2002 System" provides recommendations for functionally classifying mental retardation according to needed supports. This approach is much more useful for planning and delivering appropriate special education services than classifying mental retardation by intellectual functioning. Needed supports are identified and classified by an interdisciplinary team according to four levels of intensities: intermittent, limited, extensive, and pervasive. This system reflects the idea that expression of the impairments is strongly affected by the life arrangements of the individual.

- **What should curriculum goals for students with mental retardation emphasize?**

Not all students labeled mentally retarded have the same abilities or interests. Each student's program should be designed to fit his or her unique needs. Today there are many different educational and residential placement options available. In general, however, functional skills that will lead to the student's independence in the community and workplace should be the focus of most educational programs for individuals with mental retardation.

- **What are the most important features of effective instruction for students with mental retardation?**

There are six features of effective teaching which are based on the scientific method: a) precise definition and task analysis of the new skill to be learned, b) direct and frequent measurement of the student's performance, c) frequent opportunities for active student responding, d) immediate and systematic feedback, e) procedures for achieving the transfer of stimulus control from instructional cues or prompts to naturally occurring stimuli, and f) strategies for promoting the generalization and maintenance of newly learned skills to different, non-training situations and environments.

- **What is necessary to make inclusion an appropriate education for a student with mental retardation?**

  Simply placing a child with disabilities into a regular classroom does not guarantee that a student will be accepted socially or receive the most appropriate and needed instructional programming. Factors which may determine the success of an inclusive placement in a regular classroom include: the child's level of functioning, the teacher's ability to individualize instruction and make appropriate accommodations, the degree of support and collaboration with other professionals, the extent of parent involvement, and the level of peer maturity.

Essential Concepts

- Mental retardation is a complex concept that is difficult to define. It involves significant deficits in both intellectual functioning and adaptive behavior-both of which are difficult to measure. Even the slightest rewording in the definition can influence who is considered mentally retarded and, consequently, who is eligible for special education services. The most recent definition of mental retardation moves away from deficits within the individual toward levels of support needed in the environment for the individual to function effectively.

- Effective instructional methodologies include the use of a task analysis to target skills to be taught, direct and frequent measurement of learner's performance, instructional strategies which provide increased active student responding, use of systematic feedback, strategies for transferring stimulus control, and techniques for promoting generalization and maintenance of skills.

- Recent developments in instructional technology provide evidence that individuals with mental retardation can learn skills previously thought beyond their capability. Some children with mental retardation attend special public schools or live in institutional settings. More and more, however, are being educated in their neighborhood schools and are living in neighborhood settings where they make valuable contributions to their communities.

- Words such as helpless, unteachable, dependent, and childlike are often associated with people with mental retardation. Less often are people with mental retardation described with positive characteristics, such as hardworking, capable, independent, and productive. Yet, many children and adults with mental retardation are just that: hardworking, capable, independent, and productive members of classrooms and communities. Some individuals with mental retardation, certainly, are not as capable as others, but this same statement can be made about any group of people.

Chapter Six at a Glance

Main Topics	Key Points	Key Terms
Definitions of Mental Retardation	The AAMR 1983 definition of mental retardation includes the following criteria: significantly subaverage intellectual functioning, deficits in adaptive behavior, and manifestation during the developmental period.	mild retardation moderate retardation severe retardation profound retardation intermittent support limited support extensive support pervasive support adaptive behavior
	AAMR's new definition based on needed supports states that students with MR have significant limitations in both intellectual functioning and conceptual, social, and practical adaptive skills; and the disability originates before age 18.	
	Classification of MR according to AAMR's 1992/2002 definition is based on four levels of support: intermittent, limited, extensive, and pervasive.	
Identification and Assessment	Norm-referenced, standardized IQ tests, such as the Weschler Intelligence Scale for Children-III and the Standford-Binet IV, are used to assess intelligence.	standardized test norm referenced test normal curve standard deviation adaptive behavior scales
	A diagnosis of MR requires an IQ score at least 2 standard deviations below the mean (70 or less).	
	Although IQ scores have proven to be the single best predictor of school achievement, they have some important limitations.	
	Adaptive behavior is the effectiveness or degree with which the individual meets the standards of personal independence and social responsibility expected of his age and social group.	
	The AAMR Adaptive Behavior Scale and Vineland Adaptive Behavior Scales are commonly used to assess adaptive behavior.	
	Measurement of adaptive behavior has proven difficult because of the relative nature of social adjustment and competence.	
Prevalence	During the 1999-2000 school year, approximately 1% of the total school enrollment received special education services on the MR category.	
Causes and Prevention of Mental Retardation	More than 250 causes of MR have been identified.	prenatal perinatal postnatal psychosocial disadvantage developmental retardation amniocentesis chorion villus sampling
	Causes are categorized by the terms prenatal (e.g., chromosomal disorders, syndrome disorders), perinatal (e.g., intrauterine disorders, neonatal disorders), and postnatal (e.g., head injuries, infections, degenerative disorders, malnutrition).	
	When there is no biological evidence, the cause is presumed to be psychosocial disadvantage. Deprivation in the early years of life is the key cause of environmentally caused MR.	

Chapter Six at a Glance

Main Topics	Key Points	Key Terms
Characteristics of Students with Mental Retardation	Most students with mild MR master academic skills up to about 6th grade and are able to learn job skills well enough to support themselves independently or semi-independently.	generalization behavioral excesses
	People with moderate MR are more likely to have physical disabilities and behavior problems than are individuals with mild MR.	
	Almost always identified at birth or shortly after, most students with severe MR have significant central nervous system damage and additional disabilities or health conditions.	
	Students with mental retardation have poor memory, slower rates of learning, poor generalization, difficulty with higher-order cognitive skills, and may exhibit poor motivation.	
	Adaptive behavior deficits tend to occur across the following domains of functioning: self-care and daily living skills, social development, and behavioral excesses.	
Educational Approaches	A functional curriculum will maximize a student's independence, self-direction, and enjoyment in everyday school, home, community, and work environments.	functional curriculum life skills self-determination applied behavior analysis task analysis active student response positive reinforcement acquisition stage of learning practice stage of learning stimulus control
	Skills that will help students with MR transition into adult life in the community include a functional curriculum, life skills, and self-determination.	
	The principles of applied behavior analysis (e.g., task analysis, direct and frequent measurement, active student responding, systematic feedback) provide effective strategies for teaching students with MR.	
Educational Placement Alternatives	Although some children with MR attend special schools, most are educated in their neighborhood schools (special classes, regular class with support, or resource room).	inclusion
	The extent to which a student with MR should be included in the regular classroom should be determined by the student's individual needs.	
Current Issues and Future Trends	Two issues confronting the field of MR are a continued search for a definition and increasing the acceptance and membership of persons with MR in society.	
	An especially important and continuing challenge is moving beyond the physical integration of persons with MR in society to acceptance and membership that comes from holding valued roles.	

Guided Review _____

I. Definitions of Mental Retardation
   A. AAMR's 1983 Definition in IDEA
      • significantly subaverage _____

      • deficits in _____

      • manifested during the _____

   B. AAMR's New Definition Based on Needed Supports
      • significant limitations in both intellectual functioning and conceptual, social, and practical adaptive skills; the disability originates before age 18

      • Intensities of supports: _____

II. Identification and Assessment
   A. Assessing Intellectual Functioning
      • Norm-referenced, standardized IQ tests are used to assess intelligence.

      • A diagnosis of MR requires an IQ score of at least _____

     _____
      • IQ scores have proven to be the single best predictor of _____
      • Important considerations of IQ tests:

          IQ is a _____

          IQ tests measure how a child performs _____

          IQ tests can be _____

          IQ scores can _____

          IQ testing is not _____

          Results should never be used as the sole basis for _____

          _____

          Results from an IQ test should not be used to _____

   B. Assessing Adaptive Behavior
      • Adaptive behavior is the effectiveness or degree with which the individual meets the

      standards of _____

      • Instruments used to assess adaptive behavior include: _____

      _____

- Measurement of adaptive behavior has proven difficult because of the _____

_____

III. Prevalence
- During the 1999-2000 school year, approximately 1% of the total school enrollment received special education services in the MR category.

IV. Causes and Prevention of Mental Retardation
A. Causes
- More than 250 causes of MR have been identified.

- Etiological factors are categorized as _____

- For approximately 50% of mild MR cases and 30% of severe MR, the cause is _____

B. Biological Causes
- Specific biological causes are identified for about _____
- The term syndrome refers to a number of symptoms or characteristics that occur together and

  provide the _____

- Prenatal causes include: _____

_____

- Perinatal causes include: _____

- Postnatal causes include: _____

_____

C. Environmental Causes
- Mild MR cases make up about _____ of all persons with MR.

- In the vast majority of those cases there is no evidence of _____

- When there is no biological evidence, the cause is presumed to be _____
- Deprivation in the early years of life is the key cause of environmentally caused MR.

D. Prevention
- The biggest single preventive strike against MR was the development of _____

_____

- Toxic exposure through maternal substance abuse and environmental pollutants are two major

_____

- Advances in medical science have enabled doctors to identify certain genetic influences.
- Although early identification and intensive educational services to high-risk infants show

  promise, there is still no widely used technique to _____

_____

V. Characteristics of Students with Mental Retardation
   A. Students with Milder Forms of Mental Retardation
- Most students with mild MR master academic skills up to about 6th grade and are _____

        _____

- People with moderate MR are more likely to have _____

        _____

   B. Students with Severe Forms of Mental Retardation

- Almost always identified at _____, most students with severe

      MR have significant _____ and additional disabilities or health
      conditions.

   C. Cognitive Functioning
- Students with mental retardation have poor memory, slower rates of learning, poor generalization, and difficulty with higher-order cognitive skills, and may exhibit poor motivation.

   D. Adaptive Behavior
- Adaptive behavior deficits tend to occur across the following domains of functioning:

        _____

VI. Educational Approaches
   A. Curriculum Goals
     1. Functional Curriculum
- A functional curriculum will maximize a student's _____

            _____

     2. Life skills
- Life skills will help students with MR transition into adult life in the community.
     3. Self-determination
- Self-determined learners set goals, plan and implement a course of action, _____

            _____

- An important and initial component of self-determination is teaching students to

            _____

   B. Instructional Methodology
- Students with MR learn best when instruction is explicit and systematic.

     1. Task Analysis
- breaking down _____
     2. Direct and Frequent Measurement
- Teachers should verify the effects of their instruction _____

            _____

3. Active Student Response
   - Providing instruction with high levels of active student participation is important for all learners, especially those with disabilities.
4. Systematic Feedback
   - Feedback is generally more effective when it is _____

   _____

   - Feedback in the acquisition stage of learning should focus on _____

   - Feedback in the practice stage of learning should focus on _____
5. Transfer of Stimulus Control
   - Response prompts are gradually and systematically withdrawn.
6. Generalization and Maintenance
   - The extent to which students extend what they have learned _____

   _____

   - Aiming for natural contingencies of reinforcement means teaching skills that will be reinforced in the child's natural environment.
   - Programming common stimuli means making the teaching environment as similar as possible to the generalization setting.
   - Community-based instruction increases the probability of generalization and maintenance.

VII. Educational Placement Alternatives
   - Although some children with MR attend special schools, most are educated in _____

   _____ (special classes, regular class with support, or resource room).

   - Students with MR are usually taught _____

   _____

   - The extent to which a student with MR should be included in the regular classroom should be

   determined by _____

VIII. Current Issues and Future Trends
   A. The Evolving Definition of Mental Retardation
   Some concerns of the current definition of MR include:

   - IQ testing will remain the _____

   - Adaptive skills cannot be _____

   - The levels of needed supports are too _____

   - Classification will remain essentially _____

   Acceptance and Membership
   - An especially important and continuing challenge is moving beyond the physical integration

   of persons with MR in society to _____

   _____

In Class Activities

Small Group Activity: Identify the dimensions of effective feedback

Examine the following examples and determine which dimensions of feedback are provided: frequent, immediate, positive, specific, or differential.

1. Tyree completed 10 long division problems and brought his work to his teacher, Mr. Wei. Mr. Wei checked Tyree's work and said, "Very good, Tyree. You got 8 correct today. That's three more than yesterday!"

2. Marlene handed in a written composition. The next day her teacher circled all of the mechanical errors in red pencil, and wrote at the top of Marlene's paper, "You're making a lot of mistakes, but I liked your story."

3. When the students entered the classroom after lunch, Jordan went to her seat and immediately began writing in her journal. Her teacher said, "Jordan, you always do good work in my class."

4. While his students are working independently on their spelling assignments, Mr. Hardy monitors their progress by walking around the room and telling students which answers are correct. When students have the incorrect answers, he shows them the correct way to do the skill. He then returns to those students to check if they have successfully corrected their work.

5. During a social skills lesson, Ms. Silbernagel asks the students for examples of when it would be a good time to say, "I'm sorry." Helen answers, "tomorrow?" Ms. Silbernagel says, "Uh. OK...anyone _____ else?"

Small Group Activity: Develop a 5-day unit

Form a cooperative group for the purpose of developing a 5-day unit on a specific curricular area for a classroom in which an individual with mental retardation is included. The emphasis of your 5-day unit should be on adaptations and instructional strategies employed to ensure that the needs of the child with mental retardation are met. When developing your unit, plan to use one or more of the following active student responding techniques: choral responding, response cards, guided notes, time trials, or peer tutoring.

Homework _____

The Mismeasure of Man (1996) by Stephan J. Gould provides a cogent critique of the use of IQ tests. Among his criticisms is the tendency for "reification" or converting abstract concepts (like IQ) into measurable objects. Write a 2-page reaction paper to the following quote in the book:

> "The principal error, in fact, has involved a major theme of this book: reification-in this case, the notion that such a nebulous, socially defined concept as intelligence might be identified as a 'thing' with a locus in the brain and a definite degree of heritability-and that it might be measured as a single number, thus permitting a unilinear ranking of people according to the amount of it they possess." (pp. 268-269)

Respond to the following questions in your paper.
1. Define intelligence in your own words.
2. Can something like intelligence be measured?
3. Cultural background has been shown to affect the results of intelligence tests. What does this say about the validity of intelligence as a real entity?
4. What are the advantages and disadvantages of using intelligence tests for placing students?

What Do You Think?
Can a functional curriculum be taught effectively in inclusive classrooms?

Identifying functional curriculum goals and objectives for children with mental retardation has become a priority in special education. A functional curriculum should maximize a student's independence, self-direction, and enjoyment in school, home, community, and work environments. Write a 3-4 page position paper discussing the extent to which functional curriculum goals can be met in an inclusive regular education classroom. Under what circumstances should resource or self-contained classrooms be the placement option for instruction of functional skills?

Resources and Suggestions for Exploration

Beck, J., & Broers, J. (1994). Strategies for functional community-based instruction and inclusion for children with mental retardation. Teaching Exceptional Children, 26, 44-48.

Freemann, S. (2000). Academic and social attainments of children with mental retardation in general education and special education settings. Remedial & Special Education, 21, 3-20.

McCay, L. O., & Keyes, D. W. (2001/2002). Developing social competence in the inclusive primary classroom. Childhood Education, 78, 70-79.

O'Donoghue, T. A., & Chalmers, R. (2000). How teachers manage their work in inclusive classrooms. Teaching and Teacher Education, 16, 889-904.

Peetsma, T. (2001). Inclusion in education: Comparing pupils' development in special and regular education. Educational Review, 53, 125-136.

Sandler, A. G. (1999). Short-changed in the name of socialization? Acquisition of functional skills by students with mental retardation. Mental Retardation, 37, 148-151.

Wilson, B. A. (1999). Inclusion: Empirical guidelines and unanswered questions. Education and Training in Mental Retardation and Developmental Disabilities, 3, 119-33.

*Objectives*_____

DEFINITIONS OF MENTAL RETARDATION
1. List the components of the IDEA definition of mental retardation.
2. List the components of the AAMR's "new definition" of mental retardation.
3. List and describe the levels of needed support outlined in the "2002 system."

IDENTIFICATION AND ASSESSMENT
1. Describe the method for assessing intellectual functioning.
2. Describe the considerations when interpreting the results of IQ tests.
3. Define adaptive behavior.
4. Describe the method for assessing adaptive functioning.

PREVALENCE
1. Explain why estimating prevalence is difficult.

CAUSES AND PREVENTION OF MENTAL RETARDATION
1. List and describe the biological causes of mental retardation.
2. Describe the environmental causes of mental retardation.
3. List the types of preventive measures.

CHARACTERISTICS OF STUDENTS WITH MENTAL RETARDATION
1. Describe the common characteristics of students with mild mental retardation.
2. Describe the common characteristics of students with moderate mental retardation.
3. Describe the common characteristics of students with severe mental retardation.

EDUCATIONAL APPROACHES
1. Identify and describe the curriculum goals for students with mental retardation.
2. Identify and describe effective instructional methods for students with mental retardation.

EDUCATIONAL PLACEMENT ALTERNATIVES
1. Describe the continuum of educational placements for students with mental retardation.

CURRENT ISSUS AND FUTURE TRENDS
1. Discuss issues confronting the field of mental retardation.

*Self-check Quiz*_____

True/False

1. Joyce is a teacher. After suffering a head injury in a car accident, she has subaverage intellectual functioning and adaptive behavior deficits. She will probably not be diagnosed as mentally retarded.

2. Much of the variability in prevalence rates of mental retardation is explained by socioeconomic status.

3. Because students with mental retardation learn at a slower rate, teachers should always provide plenty of time for them to complete their work.

4. The classifications of educable mentally retarded (EMR) and trainable mentally retarded (TMR) are favored because they help teachers define achievement limits.

5. The vast majority of people with mental retardation have mild retardation and no apparent neurological or biological pathology.

6. If a traditional academic skill is not a typical activity or learning outcome for students with mental retardation, teachers should assume that it is not functional.

7. Time trials should be used only after students have learned how to do a skill correctly.

8. AAMR's 2002 definition of mental retardation emphasizes the importance of inclusive educational placements.

9. Teaching students with mental retardation to seek teacher attention and assistance when they want help is a way of fostering independence.

10. A child with Down syndrome has an IQ around the 1st percentile but becomes a television personality, demonstrating near-average functioning in the community. He probably would not be classified as mentally retarded.

11. Students in the practice stage of learning should be given feedback after every response to assure that errors are not practiced.

12. AAMR's new definition of mental retardation is the basis for radical change in state guidelines for identification.

13. Most cases of mild mental retardation are believed to be caused by factors that occur before or during birth.

14. Inclusion for children with mental retardation is most beneficial if provided in the secondary years, as a prelude to transition.

15. Intelligence test scores highly correlate with academic achievement.

Essay Questions

1. Describe the intent of curriculum goals for individuals with mental retardation, providing five examples of such goals for a fictitious child.

2. Summarize the features of applied behavior analysis.

3. Describe normalization and the related concept of social role valorization.

CHAPTER SEVEN
LEARNING DISABILITIES

Focus Questions_____

- **Why has the concept of learning disabilities proven so difficult to define?**

  There are many different types of academic and social skills students are expected to learn during their formal education and a wide range of individual differences among learners in any given classroom. No two children will learn the same skill at exactly the same rate or to the exact same level of proficiency. In one sense, all students could be said to be learning disabled in relation to some level of "standard" performance. The field of learning disabilities has struggled to describe the defining characteristics of this disability as a formal area of special education. The definition itself, however, provides the classroom teacher with little useful information about how or what to teach a particular student. The majority of educational professionals' efforts should be devoted to the development and delivery of effective instruction rather than debates over definitions.

- **Do most students who are identified as learning disabled have a true disability, or are they just low achievers or victims of poor instruction?**

  They are probably both. Learning disabilities are considered by some to be a school-defined phenomenon because the disability is most commonly exhibited through difficulties in mastering academic skills. The process of learning how to read or do mathematics is not fundamentally different from learning how to drive a car, operate a computer, drive a nail, or make a friend. While learning disabilities are often specific to certain kinds of skills, many individuals have difficulty learning across a wide range of settings and situations. The student who has experienced difficulties in learning throughout school will not magically lose this disability upon graduation. The learning disability will change only in the sense that the skills to be learned are different.

- **What are the most important skills for an elementary student with learning disabilities to master? A secondary student?**

  Instruction must continuously change to meet the changing needs of the student. As students with learning disabilities get older, different teaching settings and/or instructional priorities may be warranted. Instruction may, for example, need to focus less on basic skills and concentrate more on such skills as learning strategies and self-management techniques. The most important skills are those that meet the needs of the student at each stage of her development.

- **How do basic academic skills and learning strategies relate to each other?**

  Learning strategies are procedures a student follows when planning, executing, and evaluating performance on a task and its outcomes. In order to become proficient in the use of learning strategies, students will need at least some proficiency with the application of basic academic skills.

- **Should all students with learning disabilities be educated in the regular classroom?**

  For the majority of students with LD, the least restrictive environment is the regular classroom for all or most of the day. The movement towards full inclusion has many advocates for students with LD worried. Although the full inclusion movement has the best intentions for children with disabilities, little research supports it. Most special educators believe that the placement of students with disabilities should be determined on an individual basis.

Essential Concepts _____

- Learning disabilities are often called the "invisible disability" because there are no physical signs associated with the diagnosis, yet ironically, it is by far the largest IDEA category in terms of children served in special education.

- There is no standard, universally accepted definition of what constitutes a learning disability. However, the fundamental, defining characteristic of students with learning disabilities is: specific and significant achievement discrepancy in the presence of adequate overall intelligence.

- The causes of a specified learning disability are often unknown. Nevertheless, children with LD frequently display reading problems, deficits in written language, academic underachievement, and social skills problems, and are sometimes inattentive and hyperactive.

- Assessment is essential to planning an instructional program to teach the skills a child needs to acquire. Using assessment information to improve instruction is at the heart of "best practice" in educating students with learning disabilities. Educational approaches should focus on the child's specific skill deficit. Approaches such as curriculum-based measurement, precision teaching, explicit instruction, content enhancements, and learning strategies have been empirically supported as effective teaching strategies for students with LD.

- All children have difficulty learning at one time or another or to one degree or another. In addition, most students with LD spend at least part of the day in the general education classroom. Therefore, an understanding of LD is important for all teachers because they are likely to meet children with some type of learning problem in their own classroom one day.

Chapter Seven at a Glance

Main Topics	Key Points	Key Terms
Definitions	Although there is no universally agreed-on definition of learning disabilities, most states and school districts require three criteria be met to qualify for special education services: 1) a severe discrepancy between ability and achievement, 2) learning problems cannot be attributed to other disabilities, and 3) a need for special education services.	
Characteristics	Students with learning disabilities experience one or more of the following characteristics: reading problems, deficits in written language, underachievement in math, poor social skills, attention deficits and hyperactivity, and behavioral problems.	minimal brain dysfunction dyslexia
ADHD	The essential feature of attention deficit/hyperactivity disorder is a persistent pattern of inattention and/or hyperactivity-impulsivity.	
	Children with ADHD can be provided special education services under the "other health impairments" category.	
	Two treatment approaches widely used with children with ADHD are drug therapy and behavior modification.	
Prevalence	Learning disabilities is by far the largest of all special education categories. About half of all children receiving special education services are identified as having LD.	
	Students with LD represent about 5% of the school age population.	
Causes	In most cases of learning disabilities, there is no known cause. Four suspected causes are brain damage or dysfunction, heredity, biochemical imbalance, and environmental factors.	biochemical imbalance
	Assuming a child's learning problems are caused by a dysfunctioning brain can serve as a built-in excuse for ineffective instruction.	
	Today, most professionals in learning disabilities give little credence to biochemical imbalance as a significant cause of learning problems.	
	Impoverished living conditions early in a child's life and poor instruction probably contribute to the achievement deficits in the LD category.	
Assessment	Intelligence and achievement tests are administered to determine if there is a discrepancy between intellectual ability and achievement. Other forms of assessment are criterion-referenced tests, informal reading inventories, and direct daily measurement.	Norm-referenced tests Criterion-referenced tests curriculum-based assessment precision teaching

Chapter Seven at a Glance

Main Topics	Key Points	Key Terms
Educational Approaches	Research has shown that students with learning disabilities have difficulty organizing information on their own, bring limited stores of background knowledge to many academic activities, and often do not approach learning tasks in effective and efficient ways.	explicit instruction content enhancements guided notes learning strategies mnemonic device
	Many students' learning problems can be remediated by direct, intensive, and systematic instruction.	
	Content enhancement is the general name given to a wide range of techniques teachers use to enhance the delivery of critical curriculum content so students are better able to organize, comprehend, and retain that information. Examples of content enhancements are guided notes, graphic organizers and visual displays, and mnemonics.	
	Learning strategies help students guide themselves successfully through specific tasks or general problems.	
Educational Placement Alternatives	During the 1998-1999 school year, 43% of students with learning disabilities were educated in regular classrooms.	consultant teacher resource room
	Some school districts employ a collaborative teaching model to support the full inclusion of students with learning disabilities.	
	A consultant teacher provides support to regular classroom teachers and other school staff who work directly with students with learning disabilities. The consultant teacher helps the regular teacher select assessment devices, curriculum materials, and instructional activities.	
	A resource room is a specially staffed and equipped classroom where students with learning disabilities come for one or several periods during the school day to received individualized instruction.	
Current Issues and Future Trends	The discussion and debate over what constitutes a true learning disability are likely to continue.	
	It is important for schools to respond to the individual needs of all children with disabilities.	
	Most professionals and advocates for students with learning disabilities do not support full inclusion, which would eliminate the continuum of service delivery options.	
	Students with learning disabilities possess positive attributes and interests that teachers should identify and try to strengthen.	

Guided Review

I. Definitions
    *   In IDEA, a learning disability is defined as a disorder in _____

        _____

    *   It does not include learning problems that are the result of _____

        _____

        _____

    *   The NJCLD definition addresses the weaknesses of the IDEA definition.

    *   Most states and school districts require three criteria be met: _____

        _____

II. Characteristics
    *   Students with learning disabilities display one or more of the following characteristics: _____

        _____

        _____

III. Attention-Deficit/Hyperactivity Disorder
    *   The essential feature of ADHD is a persistent pattern of _____

        _____

    *   Children with ADHD can be served under the _____category.
    *   Estimates of prevalence of ADHD range from 3% to 5% of all school-age children.

    *   Two treatment approaches widely used for children with ADHD are _____

        _____

IV. Prevalence
    *   Learning disabilities is by far the largest of all special education categories.
    *   51% of all children with disabilities receive services under the LD category.
    *   5 out of every 100 students in the U.S. have a learning disability.

V. Causes
    A. Brain Damage or Dysfunction
        *   In most cases there is no evidence of brain damage or dysfunction.
        *   Assuming a child's learning problems are caused by a dysfunctioning brain can serve as a

            _____

    B. Heredity
        *   There is growing evidence that genetics may account for _____

            _____

C. Biochemical Imbalance
- Today, most professionals in learning disabilities give little credence to biochemical

    imbalance as a _____

D. Environmental Factors
- Impoverished living conditions early in a child's life and poor instruction _____

    _____

- Many students' learning problems can be remediated by _____

    _____

VI. Assessment
- Intelligence and achievement tests are administered to determine if there is a discrepancy between

    _____

- Other forms of assessment are _____

    _____

VII. Educational Approaches
- Research has shown that students with learning disabilities have difficulty _____

    _____

    _____

A. Explicit Instruction
- Provide students with a _____

- Provide models of proficient performance.

- Have students explain _____

- Provide frequent, positive _____

- Provide adequate _____

B. Content Enhancements
- Content enhancement is the general name given to a wide range of techniques teachers use to

    enhance the delivery of critical curriculum content so students are better able to _____

    _____

- Examples of content enhancements are _____

    _____

C. Learning Strategies
* Proficient learners approach tasks and problems _____

* Students use task-specific strategies to _____

_____

* A mnemonic device might be used to help students remember _____

_____

VIII. Educational Placement Alternatives
A. Regular Classroom
* During the 1998-1999 school year, 43% of students with learning disabilities were educated

_____

* Some school districts employ a collaborative teaching model to support _____

_____

B. Consultant Teacher
* A consultant teacher provides support to _____

_____

* The consultant teacher helps the regular teacher select _____

_____

C. Resource Room
* A resource room is a specially staffed and equipped classroom where students with learning

disabilities _____

* Some advantages of the resource room are that _____

_____

_____

* Some disadvantages are that _____

_____

_____

IX. Current Issues and Future Trends
* The discussion over what constitutes a true learning disability is likely to continue.

* It is important for schools to respond to the _____

* Most professionals and advocates for students with learning disabilities do not support _____

_____

* Students with learning disabilities possess positive attributes and interests that teachers should identify and try to strengthen.

In Class Activity

Small Group Activity: Identifying Adaptations

Get into a group of 4-5 students; then select a grade level and curricular area. You will be planning a 5-day unit for your selected class in which an individual with a learning disability is fully included. For each lesson emphasize the adaptations or modifications made to the learning environment of the child with disabilities.

Homework

1. Review the sections of this chapter on content enhancement and learning strategies. Write a lesson plan on a topic of your choice, incorporating a variety of the strategies outlined in the chapter.

2. Develop a set of guided notes that would be used with a lesson on the content area and skill level of your choice. Refer to the suggestions for creating guided notes in the chapter.

What Do You Think?
Identifying Children with Learning Disabilities

The most common practice for identifying children with learning disabilities is determining if a discrepancy exists between their ability and achievement. The discrepancy criterion is usually determined by comparing the student's IQ score to an achievement test score. There are many problems with this system of identification. According to Sternberg and Grigorenko (2001), "We should immediately stop using discrepancy scores to identify children with learning disabilities. The method is psychologically and psychometrically indefensible. It must go."(p. 339). Write a 4-5 page paper explaining some of the problems with the discrepancy criterion, and suggest alternative ways of identifying children with learning disabilities.

Resources and Suggestions for Exploration

Fletcher et al. (1998). Intelligence testing and the discrepancy model for children with learning disabilities. Learning Disabilities Research and Practice, 13, 186-203.

Fletcher, J. M., Francis, D. J., Rourke, B. P., Shaywitz, S. E., & Shaywitz, B. A. (1992). The validity of discrepancy-based definitions of reading disabilities. Journal of Learning Disabilities, 25, 555-561.

Francis, D. J., & Fletcher, J. M. (1996). Conceptual and psychometric issues with the use of IQ tests. Language, Speech, and Hearing Services in School, 27, 132-143.

Gunderson, L., & Siegel, L. S. (2001). The evils of the use of IQ tests to define learning disabilities in first- and second-language learners. Reading Teacher, 55, 48-56.

Schuerholz, L. J., & Harris, E. L. (1995). An analysis of two discrepancy-based models and a processing deficit approach in identifying learning disabilities. Journal of Learning Disabilities, 28, 18-30.

Sternberg, R. J., & Grigorenko, E. L. (2001). Learning disabilities, schooling, and society. Phi Delta Kappan, 83, 335-339.

Objectives

DEFINITIONS
1. List the components of the federal (IDEA) definition of LD.
2. List the components of the proposed NJCLD definition of LD.
3. Compare (similarities) and contrast (differences) between the two definitions.
4. List the three criteria that most states use to identify children with LD.

CHARACTERISTICS OF STUDENTS WITH LEARNING DISABILITIES
1. Describe the academic and social skills deficits associated with LD.
2. Describe the treatment options for children diagnosed with ADHD.
3. Identify the "defining characteristics" of children with LD.

PREVALENCE
1. List the prevalence estimates for children with LD.

CAUSES OF LEARNING DISABILITIES
1. Describe the four hypothesized causes of LD.
2. List the three reasons why educators should not place too much emphasis on theories linking LD with brain dysfunction.

ASSESSMENT
1. Compare and contrast the various types of assessment for LD.
2. Discuss the advantages of direct daily measurement.

EDUCATIONAL APPROACHES
1. Define and describe the major principles of effective instructional design.
2. List the characteristics of explicit instruction.
3. Provide examples of content enhancements for children with LD.
4. Provide examples of learning strategies for children with LD.

EDUCATIONAL SERVICE ALTERNATIVES
1. Identify and describe the various placement alternatives for students with LD.

CURRENT ISSUES AND FUTURE TRENDS
1. Discuss the two issues concerning the continuing debate over defining LD.
2. Discuss the need for the continuum of services for children with LD.
3. Describe the reasons for maintaining a positive focus when educating children with LD.

Self-check Quiz

True/False

1. More children are identified as learning disabled than any other IDEA category.

2. A consultant teacher may work with many regular classroom teachers, but may never actually work with students.

3. Ralph never attended school until age nine, so he is far behind his peers academically. Using IDEA criteria, it's still possible that he can be identified as learning disabled.

4. The fundamental, defining characteristic of learning disabilities is specific and significant achievement deficits in conjunction with adequate intelligence.

5. Many educators and experts contend that the ever-increasing number of children identified as learning disabled is from overidentification of low achievers.

6. The preferred treatment for children with attention-deficit/hyperactivity disorder is drug therapy.

7. Most students with learning disabilities have reading and math deficits but typical social skills.

8. Under IDEA, students with learning problems that result from an emotional disturbance cannot be identified as learning disabled.

9. Attention deficit/hyperactivity disorder is a learning disability.

10. Because of IDEA criteria, a child who is identified as learning disabled in one state would have also been identified if evaluated in another state.

11. All students with learning disabilities experience reading problems.

12. Ability-achievement discrepancy is typically measured by comparing a student's IQ score to an achievement test score to determine if they are consistent.

13. Mnemonics are increasingly used to help assess students with suspected learning disabilities.

14. Criterion-referenced tests, direct daily measurement, and curriculum-based measurement are all commonly used to assess suspected learning disabilities.

15. The primary instructional focus in educating children with learning disabilities is remediation.

Essay Questions

1. Describe the criticisms of the IDEA definition of learning disabilities that led the National Joint Committee on Learning Disabilities (NJCLD) to create their own definition.

2. Explain the importance of phonemic awareness, and provide four examples of behaviors that indicate that a child is phonemically aware.

CHAPTER EIGHT
EMOTIONAL AND BEHAVIORAL DISORDERS

Focus Questions

- **Why should a child who behaves badly be considered disabled?**

  One of the most critical factors for determining our acceptance and success in school, work, and community is our behavior. The way we behave and interact with others has a direct influence on how well we learn and perform. For example, a student who spends a large part of his day antagonizing other students, refusing to participate in class activities, and defying the teacher will probably not succeed academically. The adult who argues with co-workers, customers, and supervisors is likely to lose his or her job. Why then should children who behave badly be considered disabled? Their misconduct can interfere with their acceptance by others, their access to important opportunities, and the quality of their lives.

- **Who is more severely disabled: the acting-out, antisocial child, or the withdrawn child?**

  When attempting to determine the relative severity of a disorder, it is necessary to examine the individual child and the extent to which the behavior interferes with his or her ability to function. Acting-out children tend to be disruptive. Their emotional and behavioral disorders interfere with their acquisition of important skills. Although withdrawn children may not be disruptive, their behavior also interferes with their learning. Acting-out and withdrawn children are probably equally disabled because both encounter problems with the acquisition of academic, social, personal, and vocational skills. From an identification perspective, withdrawn children may be more disabled because they are less likely to be identified and to receive treatment.

- **How are behavior problems and academic performance interrelated?**

  There is a strong correlation between low academic achievement and behavior disorders. Behavior problems almost always lead to failure in academic performance, and a history of academic failure may predispose students to further antisocial behavior. For this reason, teachers of students with EBD must break this cycle by focusing on interventions that address both academic and behavior deficits. Improvement in behavior may create a situation more conducive to learning, while academic success may decrease behavior problems.

- **How can a teacher's efforts to defuse a classroom disturbance actually escalate a misbehavior?**

  Some teachers of students with EBD create an environment in which coercion is the primary means for controlling inappropriate behavior. Coercive environments promote escape and avoidance by those being coerced. Teachers of students with emotional and behavioral disorders must strive to design classroom environments that are effective for decreasing anti-social behavior and increasing the frequency of positive teacher-student interactions.

- **What are the most important skills for teachers of students with emotional and behavioral disorders?**

  All teachers, including those who teach students with EBD, must be skilled in delivering effective instruction so that students will attain mastery of important academic and social skills. The most effective teachers will create positive, supportive environments that promote and maintain student success. Teachers of students with emotional and behavioral disorders must have good problem-solving skills and be prepared for the challenge of managing and changing disruptive behaviors.

Essential Concepts

- Rhode, Jenson, and Reavis (1999) describe children with emotional and behavioral problems as "tough kids." Perhaps no other label describes them so well. Many of them have few friends and often behave in such a persistently obnoxious manner that they seem to invite negative responses from peers and adults. However, anyone who has ever taught "tough kids" will tell you that they can be bright, creative, energetic, and even fun to be around under the right circumstances.

- This chapter begins with a discussion of the federal (IDEA) and alternate (CCBD) definitions of Emotional and Behavioral Disorders. Although the IDEA definition provides the foundation for receiving specialized services, there are many troubling aspects of the definition, not the least of which is that the definition disqualifies many of the children who would benefit from special education. In response, the Council for Children with Behavior Disorders (CCBD) proposed an alternate definition of emotional and behavioral disorders as a disability characterized by "behavioral or emotional responses in school programs so different from appropriate age, cultural, or ethnic norms that they adversely affect educational performance."

- Boys are as much as four times more likely to be given the label of EBD than girls. Most children with EBD exhibit externalizing behaviors (e.g., noncompliance, aggression, tantrums), but many exhibit internalizing behaviors (e.g., excessive shyness, depression). Because children who manifest internalizing behaviors may be less disturbing to others than children who emit externalizing behaviors, they are in danger of underidentification.

- The causes of EBD are poorly understood, and estimates of the number of children with EBD vary widely. Nevertheless, explanations for the causes of EBD generally tend to fall into two categories, biological or environmental. Biological factors may include heredity and temperament. Environmental factors include home, community, peers, and school.

- Identification and assessment should be conducted as early as possible. Most screening devices usually consist of behavioral rating scales and teacher checklists. However, with the renewal of IDEA (1997), increased emphasis has been placed on direct measurement of behavior as exemplified by functional behavioral assessment (FBA).

- In order for children with EBD to become productive members of society, curriculum and instruction must focus primarily on academics and self-management skills. Research indicates that improving academic performance also has collateral effects on social skills. However, improvements in social skills do not usually correlate with improved academic performance. Whatever the focus, teachers should remember to concentrate on alterable variables-aspects of the environment that make a difference in the student's life and can be affected by teaching practices.

- Effective teaching practices for students with EBD include a positive proactive approach to classroom management, clear rules and behavioral expectations, the systematic use of teacher praise, and high levels of active student responding (ASR). Recent efforts aimed at schoolwide positive behavioral support may also help to remediate many behavioral problems.

Chapter Eight at a Glance

Main Topics	Key Points	Key Terms
Defining Emotional and Behavioral Disorders	The IDEA definition identifies the following conditions for a student to qualify for special education services: severity, chronicity, and difficulty in school. The CCBD definition clarifies the educational dimensions of the disability, focuses direction on behavior in school settings, and places behavior in the context of ethnic and cultural norms.	chronicity severity
Characteristics	The most common pattern of children with EBD is externalizing behaviors such as aggression and noncompliance. A pattern of antisocial behavior early in a child's development is the best single predictor of delinquency in adolescence. Children with internalizing behavior disorders have too little social interaction, and tend to be withdrawn and depressed. Children with internalizing behavior disorders (withdrawn, depressed, anxious) are in more danger of not being identified. Most students with EBD perform academically at least one or more years below grade level, and perform in the slow learner range on IQ tests (mean = 86).	externalizing behavior internalizing behavior
Prevalence	Estimates of the number of students with EBD vary widely (from 1%–10%). Far fewer children with EBD are receiving special education services than the most conservative prevalence estimates.	delinquent recidivist
Causes	Theories and conceptual models of EBD include biological factors (brain disorders, genetics, temperament) and environmental factors (home, community, school).	brain dygenesis temperament coercive pain control
Identification and Assessment	Children with suspected EBD can be evaluated using screening tests, projective tests, and/or direct observation and measurement of behavior. Behavior can be measured objectively along the following dimensions: rate, magnitude, duration, latency, and topography. Functional behavioral assessment examines behavior in the context of antecedent and consequent events for the purpose of designing interventions.	projective tests latency topography functional behavioral assessment functional analysis

Chapter Eight at a Glance

Main Topics	Key Points	Key Terms
Educational Approaches	The curriculum for students with EBD includes instruction in both academic and social skills.	proactive strategies
	Behavior management interventions include discipline and schoolwide systems of behavior support, classroom management, self-management, and peer mediation.	shaping
		contingency contracting
		extinction
	Teachers must possess differential acceptance and an empathetic relationship to deal effectively with students with EBD.	differential reinforcement
		response cost
		time out
	Special educators must focus their efforts on those aspects of the student's life they can effectively control (alterable variables).	self-monitoring
		self-evaluation
		differential acceptance
		empathetic relationship
		alterable variables
Educational Placement Alternatives	Students with EBD typically receive special education services in self-contained or resource classrooms.	
	Nearly half of all students with EBD spend at least part of the school day in regular classrooms.	
	Most students receiving special education because of EBD have serious problems that require intensive interventions in highly structured environments.	
Current Issues and Future Trends	All students with severe behavior problems need to be eligible to receive special education services.	manifestation determination
	Efforts to prevent EBD need to be increased through early screening, identification, and intervention.	wraparound services
	It is necessary to develop valid and reliable methods for conducting manifestation determinations required by IDEA disciplinary provisions.	
	Services for youth in juvenile corrections systems need to be improved.	
	"Wraparound" systems of comprehensive care can increase the likelihood that students with EBD will have their needs met. The most effective wraparound programs are characterized by child- and family-centered interventions and supports, interagency cooperation, and individualized care.	

Guided Review

I. Definitions: a clear definition of behavioral disorders is lacking because
    •   disordered behavior is a social construct.
    •   concepts and terminology used across theories can be inconsistent.
    •   there are different expectations for appropriate behavior across ethnic and cultural groups.
    •   emotional problems sometimes occur in conjunction with other disabilities.

    A. IDEA Definition: the three conditions that must be met under the IDEA definition are

        1. _____: over a long period of time

        2. _____: to a marked degree

        3. _____: adversely affects educational performance

    B. CCBD Definition of Emotional or Behavioral Disorders
        • behavioral or emotional responses so different from appropriate age, cultural, or ethnic norms they adversely affect educational performance; co-exist with other disabilities; include sustained disorders of conduct or adjustment affecting educational performance.

        • The proposed definition clarifies _____ ,

        focuses directly on _____ ,

        places behavior in the context of _____ ,

        increases the possibility of _____ ,
        and does not require distinctions between social and emotional adjustment.

II. Characteristics
    A. Externalizing Behaviors: antisocial behaviors
        • Examples of externalizing behaviors: _____

        _____

        • _____ is the "king-pin" behavior around which other behavioral excesses evolve.
        • A pattern of antisocial behavior early in a child's development is the best single predictor of

        _____

    B. Internalizing Behaviors: too little social interaction with others
        • Examples of internalizing behaviors _____

        _____

        • Without identification and effective treatment, the extreme emotional disorders of some

        children can lead to _____

    C. Academic Achievement
        • Most students with EBD perform at least one or more years below their grade level and exhibit significant deficiencies in reading and math achievement.

        • There is a strong correlation between _____

D. Intelligence
 •   Many children with EBD score in the _____
     on IQ tests.
 •   It is almost certain that the disturbed child's inappropriate behavior has interfered with

     _____

E. Social Skills and Interpersonal Relationships
 •   Students with EBD reported lower levels of empathy toward others, participation in fewer
     curricular activities, less frequent contact with friends, and lower-quality relationships than
     were reported by their peers without disabilities

III. Prevalence
 •   Estimates of children with EBD vary widely (between 1% to 10% of school-age children)

 •   Such varying estimates suggest that _____

     _____

 •   Although EBD ranked as the fourth-largest disability category in special education, most children
     with EBD are not receiving special education services.

A. Gender
 •   The vast majority of children identified for special education because of EBD are _____

 •   Boys are more likely to have externalizing disorders such as _____

 •   Girls are more likely to show internalizing disorders such as _____

B. Juvenile Delinquency
 •   Juveniles, who comprise about 20% of the total population, were involved in 16% of all violent
     crimes and 32% of all property crime arrests in 1999.
 •   About half of all juvenile delinquents are _____

IV. Causes
A. Biological Factors
    1. Brain Disorders
       •   For the vast majority of children with EBD, there is no evidence of brain disorder.
    2   Genetics
       •   The disorder with the strongest support for a genetic risk factor is _____
    3. Biologically Determined Temperament.
    4. Environmental Factors
       •   Three primary environmental factors that contribute to the development of conduct
           disorders and antisocial behavior are:

           _____

           _____

           _____

B. A Complex Pathway of Risks
  • Most behavior problems are the accumulated effect of exposure to a variety of:

     _____

V. Identification and Assessment
  • The primary purpose of initial assessment is to see whether the child's behavior is different enough

  • to _____

A. Screening Tests
  • Children identified through a screening process undergo more thorough assessment to
     determine their eligibility for special education.
     1. Behavior Rating Profile (BRP2)
     2. Child Behavior Checklist (CBCL)
     3. Systematic Screening for Behavioral Disorders (SSBD)
     4. Behavioral and Emotional Rating Scale (BERS)

B. Projective Tests
  • Consist of ambiguous stimuli (e.g., Rorschach Test) or open-ended tasks. It is assumed that
     responses to items that have no right or wrong answer will reveal a person's true personality.

C. Direct Observation and Measurement of Behavior.
  • Behavior can be measured objectively along several dimensions: _____

     _____

D. Functional Behavioral Assessment
  • FBA is a systematic process of gathering information to help IEP teams understand why a
     student is engaging in challenging behavior.
  • Two major types of behavioral function are _____

     and _____
  • The information is then used to guide the development of an intervention plan.
  • Functional analysis is _____

     _____

VI. Educational Approaches
  A. Curriculum Goals
  B. Social Skills
  C. Academic Skills
  D. Behavior Management
     1. Discipline and School-wide Systems of Behavior Support
        • Schools that implement school-wide systems of positive behavior support use

           _____

     2. Classroom Management
        • The majority of classroom behavior problems can be prevented by proactive behavior
           management.

        • Proactive strategies include _____

           _____

           _____

3. Self-Management
   - Self-management can help students learn responsibility and _____

   Self-monitoring is a procedure in which the student observes and _____

   _____

   - Self-evaluation involves _____

4. Peer Mediation and Support
   - peer monitoring: _____
   - positive peer reporting: _____
   - peer tutoring: _____
   - peer confrontation: _____

E. Fostering Strong Teacher-Student Relationships
   - Differential acceptance means _____

   _____

   - Having an empathetic relationship with a child refers to a teacher's ability to _____

   _____

F. A Focus on Alterable Variables
   - Bloom (1980) uses the term alterable variables to refer to _____

   _____

VII. Educational Placement Alternatives
   - Slightly more than half of all students with EBD receive their education in separate classrooms, special schools, and residential facilities.
   - Most students receiving special education because of emotional or behavioral disorders have

   serious, longstanding problems that require _____

VIII. Current Issues and Future Trends
   A. Serving All Students with Emotional and Behavior Disorders
   B. Preventing Emotional and Behavioral Disorders
   C. Disciplining Students with Disabilities
   D. Improving Services for Youth in Juvenile Corrections Systems
   E. Developing "Wraparound" Systems of Comprehensive Care
   F. Challenges, Achievements, and Advocacy

In Class Activities

Small Group Activity: Develop a Classroom Management Plan

Select a specific grade-level you will teach, and develop an appropriate classroom management plan for your students. When developing your classroom management plan, be sure to focus on the prevention of problem behaviors. Decide on appropriate, feasible rules and consequences. Your classroom management plan should contain the following:

Classroom Rules: Select no more than 5 rules and state them positively (i.e., what the student will do instead of what the student will not do).

Consequences for Appropriate Behavior: Select appropriate reinforcers for your students such as social (e.g., praise), tangible (e.g., stickers), activity (e.g., playing a computer game), privilege (e.g., excused from homework), and/or generalized reinforcers (e.g., tokens to be exchanged later for tangible reinforcers). Also, consider incorporating group contingencies.

Consequences for Inappropriate Behavior: Select appropriate consequences for noncompliance of the classroom rules such as response cost (e.g., losing a portion of free time), time out (e.g., removing the student from a reinforcing activity), and/or presentation of an aversive stimuli (e.g., a phone call to the parent).

Classroom Procedures: Effective classroom procedures must be directly taught, modeled, and practiced. Teaching specific procedures and routines will aid in the prevention of problem behaviors by increasing instructional time, reducing transition time, and decreasing disruptions.
What are students expected to do when they enter the classroom?
What are your procedures for beginning a class period?
What procedures should the students follow when they want to ask for help?
What is your procedure for getting the students' attention?
What is the procedure for dismissal?
What other procedures will make your classroom run more smoothly?

Small Group Activity: Conduct a Functional Assessment and Develop an Intervention Plan

Your team is assigned to develop an intervention plan for Jamal. Jamal's general education teacher has indicated that he often gets into arguments with peers, calls other students derogatory names, and is always "clowning around" in class. Your direct observations indicate that arguments with peers generally occur on the playground when Jamal wants to join an activity, and usually result in his being allowed to play. Derogatory name-calling often occurs during lunch when Jamal is sitting near peers and results in the peer calling him a derogatory name in return. Clowning around often occurs during teacher lecture time and results in peer laughter. Develop an intervention based on these results. In your plan include:

Statement of the problem behaviors
The likely function of the behaviors
Functionally equivalent desired behaviors
A plan for teaching Jamal the functionally equivalent desired behavior

Response Card Activity: Identify the Measurable Dimensions of Behavior

Select the dimension of behavior-**frequency** (or **rate**), **duration**, **latency**, **magnitude**, or **topography** illustrated in each of the following examples.

1. Marsha speaks too quietly to be understood. Ms. Simmons is teaching her to speak more loudly.

2. Mr. Flynt is trying to reduce the number of times Jimmy yells out in class.

3. Ms. Jones wants to see how long it takes Patti to get started on her math assignment.

4. Mr. Walters is trying to increase the length of time Amy stays on task when working on assignments independently.

5. Ms. Scott is trying to increase the number of math problems Michael can do in ten minutes.

6. Ms. Vance cannot read David's writing because he doesn't press hard enough with his pencil when he writes.

7. Donna often tantrums for an extended period of time. Ms. Kellum is implementing a behavior change program to reduce the length of time of Donna's tantrums.

8. Ms. Mire wants to decrease the length of time it takes Eliza to begin her spelling assignment.

9. Ms. Hampton is trying to increase the number of times Jerry asks for help with his work.

10. When Steven's teacher tells him to begin his work, Steven usually digs through his desk looking for a pencil, plays with his baseball cards, talks to the student next to him, and draws pictures on his worksheet before he finally starts on his work.

11. Ms. Cuervas is charting the number of words Melissa can read per minute.

12. Ms. Mire is using physical prompting to teach Eliza to throw a ball.

13. Mr. Mills wants to increase the number of positive social interactions Marvin has with his peers. _____

14. Mr. Carroll is doing fluency-training activities to increase the number of words Sheryl writes per minute so she can keep up with the rest of the class when taking notes.

15. Kate always slams the door loudly when entering the classroom.

16. Ms. Ladner is using a behavior management plan to help Emily reduce the number of times she _ uses profanity per class period.

17. Ms. McLaurin is timing the number of minutes Ricardo spends socially interacting with his peers.

18. Ms. Smith is gradually increasing the amount of time she requires Gary to read silently.

Response Card Activity: Identify the Functions of Behavior

Select the likely function of the behaviors **Attention, Escape, Access to Tangible** illustrated in each of the following examples.

1. Jamie is sent out of reading class for kicking Jenny's desk. The next day he is sent out of class for pulling Susan's hair.

2. Susan raises her hand to ask a question about a math assignment and the teacher answers her question. Two minutes later she raises her hand to ask if she answered the first question correctly and the teacher comes over to her desk.

3. Cheryl grabs a toy from another student and keeps the toy. During snack time she takes another student's milk and drinks it. Later she asks the teacher for a crayon and is given the crayon.

4. Enrique finishes his work quickly, making careless mistakes, so he can go outside.

5. Before going to basketball practice, Charles completes a standardized achievement test in 5 minutes by making an interesting pattern in his scantron sheet.

6. Jillian hits Greg's leg and he asks her to stop. At recess she tells a friend to push her into Greg.

7. Kevin lies to his mom and doesn't get into trouble.

8. Mrs. Crabapple saves coupons for her favorite ice cream. Later she uses the coupons to help her buy ice cream.

9. AJ cuts in the movie line to get a good seat.

10. Helene has a temper tantrum whenever she is asked to clean her room. As a result, she is rarely asked to clean her room.

11. Carlos sticks his finger in his mouth during lunch time to gross out his friends. In math class he stabs himself with a pencil and asks the teacher for a bandage.

12. Sherry cleans the house, does the dishes, and cooks dinner so her mother won't yell at her for bringing home a bad report card.

Homework

Write a 2 page position paper on either of the following topics

1. About 43% of the children receiving specialized services for emotional and behavioral disorders have a diagnosis of ADHD. Research indicates that stimulant medication is effective for treating ADHD-related symptoms (impulsivity, hyperactivity, and inattention). However, the data on the effects of medication on social and academic skills are less clear. A recent article by Forness, Kavale, Crenshaw, and Sweeny (2000), leading authorities on behavior disorders, claimed that **not** using stimulants to treat ADHD verges on educational malpractice. Should stimulant medication be a "treatment of choice" for students with ADHD? What responsibilities does the teacher have in the process of determining treatment options? What responsibilities does the teacher have in ensuring that stimulant medication is an effective treatment in terms of both social and academic performance?

2. It has been suggested that one reason schools do not use systematic screening and identification methods for suspected emotional and behavioral disorders is that many more children would be identified and that this would create a financial burden to the school. Do you think that this is a valid claim? Would you feel the same if you were a member of the school board? The principal?

What Do You Think?

Manifestation Determination: To what extent and under what circumstances should students with disabilities be disciplined in the same way as their nondisabled peers?

The discipline provisions of IDEA 1997 have presented controversy among educators and concerns about the rights of students with disabilities. Under IDEA 1997 the principal can unilaterally suspend a student with disabilities for up to 10 school days. If a student is suspended for more than 10 school days, the IEP team must hold a manifestation determination hearing to determine if there is a relationship between the misbehavior and the disability. To make this determination, the IEP team must answer the following questions and base their answers on student evaluation data.
1. Were the student's IEP and placement appropriate?
2. Was the IEP implemented as it was written?
   If the committee decides that the answer to either of these questions is "no," they conclude that a relationship exists between the disability and the misconduct. If the answer to both questions is "yes," the IEP team must ask the following:
3. Did the disability impair the student's understanding of the impact of the consequences of the behavior?
4. Did the disability impair the student's ability to control his or her misbehavior?
   If the answer to these two questions is "yes," the committee concludes there is a relationship between the disability and the misconduct. If the answer is "no," the school can discipline the student in the same way as nondisabled students (expulsion or long-term suspension). If a student is expelled or suspended long term, he or she must continue to receive a free appropriate public education in an interim alternative educational setting (IAES) and continue to work on IEP goals and objectives.

Walther-Thomas, C., & Brownell, M. T. (1998). An interview with Dr. Mitchell Yell: Changes in IDEA regarding suspension and expulsion. Intervention in School & Clinic, 34, 46-50.

The Assignment

Write a position paper stating whether or not you agree with the discipline provisions in IDEA 1997. Examine the aspects of the law that you think are appropriate and inappropriate. If you believe that any part of the law should be changed, explain the changes you would make. Additionally, provide examples of hypothetical cases in which misconduct is related and is not related to the student's disability (e.g., a seventh grader with learning disabilities is caught selling drugs at school, a ninth grader with EBD brings a hunting knife to school). Explain what information you would need to decide if the misconduct was related to the disability.

Related Issues to Consider
- Should principals be allowed to unilaterally suspend or remove students with disabilities for up to 10 days? If so, under what circumstances?
- How can a committee determine whether or not a behavior is a manifestation of the disability?
- Can IEP goals and objectives really be met in an interim alternative educational setting?

Resources and Suggestions for Exploration

Suspension and Expulsion
http://www.ppmd.org/publications/suspension_and_expulsion.html

IDEA advocates wage battle against discipline amendments
http://www.findarticles.com/cf_0/m0BSC/26_11/76938095/p1/article.jhtml?term=IDEA+discipline

Overview of the Major Discipline Provisions in the 1999 IDEA Regulations
http://www.fape.org/idea/discipline_overview.htm

Strategies to Meet IDEA 1997's Discipline Requirements
http://www.cec.sped.org/bk/focus/1297.html

Commonwealth of Virginia Department of Education v. Riley
http://www.ideapractices.org/litlog/vavriley.htm

Honig v. Doe
http://www.ideapractices.org/litlog/honigvdoe.htm

Make It, Use It
Reread the TEACHING & LEARNING IN SCHOOLS segment on using response cards to increase active participation and achievement. Create a lesson plan and develop pre-printed response cards you could use to increase ASR.

Objectives

DEFINING EMOTIONAL AND BEHAVIORAL DISORDERS
1. List the components of the federal (IDEA) definition of Emotional Disturbance.
2. List the components of the proposed (CCBD) definition of Emotional and Behavior Disorders.
3. Compare (similarities) and contrast (differences) between the two definitions.
4. Describe the problems with both the federal and proposed definition.

CHARACTERISTICS OF CHILDREN WITH EBD
1. Define and provide examples of externalizing behaviors.
2. Define and provide examples of internalizing behaviors.
3. Describe the academic and social prognosis of children with EBD.

PREVALENCE
1. List the prevalence figures for children with EBD.
2. In relation to the definition of EBD, discuss why prevalence data are difficult to determine, and discuss how this impacts children in need of specialized services.

CAUSES OF EMOTIONAL AND BEHAVIORAL DISORDERS
1. Identify and provide examples of the two likely causes of EBD.
2. Describe the factors that place a student at risk for being identified with EBD.

IDENTIFICATION AND ASSESSMENT
1. Compare and contrast the various types of assessment for EBD.
2. Define and provide examples of five measurable dimensions of behavior.
3. Discuss the advantages of assessment that uses direct observation of measurable behavior.

EDUCATIONAL APPROACHES
1. Discuss the curriculum goals for children with EBD.
2. Discuss the importance of reinforcement-based, proactive classroom management strategies.
3. Describe the components of a school-wide system of positive behavioral support.
4. Discuss the importance of teaching self-management skills.
5. Define and describe peer-mediated support.
6. Define and describe alterable variables in relation to teaching students with EBD.
7. Describe the affective traits of good teachers.

EDUCATIONAL PLACEMENT ALTERNATIVES
1. Describe the continuum of educational placements for students with EBD.

CURRENT ISSUS AND FUTURE TRENDS
1. Discuss five problem areas for providing effective appropriate educational services for students with EBD.

Self-check Quiz

True/False

1. A child who is socially maladjusted is, by IDEA standards, emotionally disordered.

2. The single best predictor of delinquency in adolescence is a pattern of antisocial behavior as a preschooler.

3. It is not necessary to understand the etiology (cause) of a student's emotional or behavioral disorder in order to effectively serve that student.

4. Compared to other disabilities, children with emotional and behavioral disorders tend to be served in less restrictive settings.

5. A child who exhibits superior academic achievement can be identified as emotionally disordered, given IDEA and CCBD definitions.

6. The use of response cards increases active participation for emotionally disordered students.

7. The purpose of screening is to identify children who qualify for special education services.

8. The number of children served under IDEA for emotional disturbance indicates that an under-identification of these children is occurring.

9. Girls are less likely than boys to be identified for special education for emotional or behavioral disorders, because physical differences make them less of a visible threat to school personnel.

10. Data on juvenile delinquents indicate that only about 60% of criminal acts by juveniles are reported, making the extent of juvenile crime unknown.

11. Biological factors, particularly temperament, are a likely cause of most emotional and behavioral disorders.

12. Children with internalizing disorders are more likely to be underidentified than those with externalizing disorders.

13. Observations are too subjective to be a useful part of assessment.

14. The most important aspect in an effective classroom management program is that the teacher react immediately and consistently to inappropriate behaviors.

15. Fewer than 20% of students with emotional or behavioral disorders receive services in special schools or residential placements.

Essay Questions

1. For a fictitious student with a behavioral disorder, write a history in which you illustrate three factors that may have contributed to the formation of his disability.

2. What components do most definitions of emotional and behavioral disorders have in common?

CHAPTER NINE
COMMUNICATION DISORDERS

Focus Questions

- **How are speech and language interrelated?**

Language is a formalized code used by a group of people to communicate with one another. Each language has rules of phonology, morphology, syntax, semantics, and pragmatics that describe how users put sounds and ideas together to convey meaning. Speech is the oral production of language. It is the fastest and most efficient method of communication by language and is also one of the most complex and difficult human endeavors. Children with impaired speech have difficulty producing sounds properly, while children with impaired language have problems understanding or using the symbols and rules people use to communicate with each other.

- **How should a teacher respond to a child who says, "The dogs runned in home."? And to a child who says, "That foop is dood!"?**

Children's words and sentences often differ from adult forms while children are learning language. As their language develops, children will gradually replace incorrect word pronunciations and sentence structures with acceptable adult forms of language. Whether or not the child's language errors are age-appropriate, it is important that the teacher respond to the child's message first before attempting to correct the errors. The teacher can respond to the child's message while modeling correct forms by saying something like, "Really? The dogs ran in the house?" or "I'm glad you think that soup is good." There are a variety of approaches for treating speech and language problems, but speech-language pathologists are increasingly employing naturalistic interventions to help children develop and use language skills.

- **What are common elements of effective interventions for speech and language impairments?**

A wide variety of approaches have been used to successfully treat speech and language impairments. No matter what the approach to treatment, children with language disorders need to be around children and adults with something interesting to talk about. Language is an interactive, interpersonal process, and naturally occurring interventions should be used to expose children with language disorders to a wide range of stimuli, experiences, contexts, and people. Effective speech-language pathologists establish specific goals and objectives, keep precise records of their students' performance, and arrange the learning environment so that each child's efforts at communication will be rewarded and enjoyable.

- **What are the most important functions of alternative and augmentative communication?**

Augmentative and alternative communication refers to a diverse set of strategies and methods to assist individuals who are unable to meet their communication needs through speech or writing. The three components of AAC are: a representational symbol set (individually selected vocabulary represented by symbols such as those included in Picture Communication Symbols, Pictogram Ideagram Communication, or Blissymbolics); a means for selecting symbols (e.g., direct selection, scanning, or encoding responses); and a means for transmitting symbols (e.g., a communication board, Prentke Romich Liberator, or DECtalk).

Why are naturalistic interventions more likely to result in maintenance and generalization of a child's new speech and language skills?

Naturalistic interventions occur in real or simulated activities that occur naturally in the home, school, or community environments in which a child normally functions. Naturalistic interventions (also known as *milieu* teaching strategies) are characterized by their use of dispersed learning trials, attempts to base teaching on the child's attentional lead within the context of normal conversational interchanges, and orientation toward teaching the form and content of language in the context of normal use. Naturalistic approaches are more likely to promote generalization of language skills because instruction occurs in the context of the child's normal daily interactions. This eliminates the step of having to carry over skills learned in didactic, contrived situations to natural situations.

Essential Concepts

- Communication is necessary in nearly every aspect of a child's day-to-day routine-its role in learning social and academic skills is critical. Disorders involving a student's articulation, voice quality, fluency, or use and understanding of language can significantly influence the student's learning. It is no wonder that speech and language disorders represent the second largest disability category in terms of the number of children served.

- Normal language development follows a relatively predictable sequence. Most children learn to use language without direct instruction by age 5. When a child's language development deviates from the norm to such an extent that he or she has serious difficulties in learning and in interpersonal relations, the child is said to have a communication disorder. Special education is needed when a communication disorder adversely affects educational performance.

- As many as 5% of school-age children have speech impairments serious enough to warrant attention. Nearly twice as many boys as girls have speech impairments. Children with articulation problems represent the largest category of speech-language impairments.

- Communication disorders that are organic are attributed to a specific physical cause. Most communication disorders, however, do not have a known physical origin. Environmental influences, such as the child's opportunity to learn speech and language, are thought to be the major causes of many communication disorders.

- There are various treatment approaches to speech and language disorders. With few exceptions, treatment of children with such disorders involves aspects of their environment where they need to communicate. The goal of most treatment programs is to teach children to communicate with a variety of other individuals and across a variety of circumstances.

- Augmentative and alternative communication (AAC) may be necessary in severe situations. An augmentative communication system is designed to supplement and enhance a person's communication capabilities.

Chapter Nine at a Glance

Main Topics	Key Points	Key Terms
Definitions	Communication involves encoding, transmitting, and decoding messages.	paralinguistic codes
	Language is a formalized code used by a group of people to communicate with one another.	nonlinguistic cues
	The five dimensions of language are phonology, morphology, syntax, semantics, and pragmatics.	phonology
	Knowledge of normal language development can help the special educator determine whether a particular child is simply developing language at a slower-than-normal rate or whether the child shows an abnormal pattern of language development.	morphology
		syntax
		semantics
		pragmatics
	Most children follow a relatively predictable sequence in their acquisition of speech and language.	phonation
	ASHA defines a communication disorder as an impairment in the ability to receive, send, process, and comprehend concepts of verbal, nonverbal, and graphic symbols systems.	resonation
		articulation
	Speech is impaired when it deviates so far from the speech of other people that it calls attention to itself, interferes with communication, or provokes distress in the speaker or listener. Three basic types of speech impairments are articulation disorders, fluency disorders, and voice disorders.	expressive language disorder
		receptive language disorder
	It is always important to keep the speaker's age, education, and cultural background in mind when determining whether speech is impaired.	dialects
	The way each of us speaks is the result of a complex mix of influences including race and ethnicity, socioeconomic class, education, occupation, geographical region, and peer group identification. Every language contains a variety of forms called dialects.	
Prevalence	A little more than 2% of school-age children receive special education for speech and language impairments, the second largest disability category under IDEA.	
	Children with articulation and spoken language problems represent the largest category of speech-language impairments.	
Causes	Most communication disorders are not considered organic but are classified as functional.	functional communication
	Factors that contribute to language disorders include cognitive limitations or mental retardation, hearing impairments, behavioral disorders, and environmental deprivation.	cleft palate
		dysarthria
		aphasia

Chapter Nine at a Glance

Main Topics	Key Points	Key Terms
Characteristics	The four basic kinds of sound speech errors are distortions, substitutions, omissions, and additions.	distortions
	A severe articulation disorder is present when a child pronounces many sounds so poorly that her speech is unintelligible most of the time.	substitutions
		omissions
	Children with phonological disorders are especially at risk in spelling and reading.	additions
		fluency disorders
	Stuttering and cluttering are examples of fluency disorders.	cluttering
		dysphonia
	Dysphonia describes any condition of poor or unpleasant voice quality.	hypernasality
		hyponasality
	A phonation disorder causes the voice to sound breathy, hoarse, husky, or strained most of the time. Resonance disorders are hypernasality or hyponasality.	
Identification and Assessment	Evaluation components include case history and physical examination, articulation test, hearing test, auditory discrimination test, phonological awareness and processing, vocabulary and language development, language samples, and observation in natural settings.	
Educational Approaches	The speech-language pathologist is the school-based professional with the primary responsibility for identifying, evaluating, and providing therapeutic services.	naturalistic interventions
		milieu teaching strategies
	Methods for treating speech and language disorders include discrimination and production activities, principles of self-monitoring, direct vocal rehabilitation, exploration of expressive language, and naturalistic interventions.	AAC
		symbol systems
	Augmentative and alternative communication have three components: a representational symbol set, a means for selecting symbols, and a means for transmitting symbols.	
Educational Placement Alternatives	89% of children with speech and language impairments are served in regular classrooms, 6.5% in resource rooms, and 4.5% in separate classes.	
	The following service delivery models are used within these three placements: monitoring, pullout, collaborative consultation, classroom-based, self-contained classroom, and community-based.	
Current Issues and Future Trends	Speech-language professionals will deal with the controversy as to whether services should take a therapeutic versus an educational focus.	
	Across-the-day interventions mean that interventions must be applicable not only in the classroom but by teachers and parents.	

Guided Review

I. Definitions
    A. Communication involves encoding, transmitting, and decoding messages.

   - Communication has the following important functions: _____

     _____

   - Paralinguistic codes include _____

   - Nonlinguistic cues include _____

   B. Language is a formalized code used by a group of people to communicate with one another.

   - The five dimensions of language are _____

     _____

   C. Speech is the oral production of language.
   - Speech sounds are the product of the following four separate but related processes:

     _____

   D. Normal Development of Speech and Language
   - Knowledge of normal language development can help the special educator determine whether

     a particular child is simply developing language at a slower-than-normal rate or _____

     _____

   - Most children follow a relatively predictable sequence in their acquisition of _____

     _____

   E. Communication Disorders Defined
       ASHA defines a communication disorder as an impairment in the ability to receive, send, process,

       and comprehend concepts of _____
    1. Speech Impairments
   - Speech is impaired when it deviates so far from the speech of other people that it _____

     _____

     _____

   - Three basic types of speech impairments are _____

     _____

   - It is always important to keep the speaker's age, education, and cultural background in
     mind when determining whether speech is impaired.

2.   Language Disorders
  - Language disorders may involve the form, content, and/or function of language in communication.
  - Children who have difficulty understanding language have a _____ language disorder.
  - Children who have difficulty producing language have an _____ language disorder.

F. Communication differences are not disorders.
  - The way each of us speaks is the result of a complex mix of influences including _____

    _____

    _____

  - Every language contains a variety of forms called _____

II. Prevalence
  - A little more than 2% of school-age children receive special education for speech and language impairments, the second largest disability category under IDEA.
  - Nearly twice as many boys as girls have speech impairments.
  - Children with articulation and spoken language problems represent the largest category of speech-language impairments.

III. Causes
  - Most communication disorders are not considered organic but are classified as _____
A. Causes of Speech Disorders
  - Physical causes include _____

    _____

  - Dysarthria refers to a group of speech disorders caused by _____

B. Causes of Language Disorders
  - Factors that contribute to language disorders include _____

  - Aphasia describes a loss of the ability to _____

IV. Characteristics
A. Speech Sound Errors
  - The four basic kinds of sound speech errors are _____

    _____

  - A severe articulation disorder is present when a child pronounces many sounds so poorly that

    her speech is _____

  - Children with phonological disorders are especially at risk in _____

B. Fluency Disorders
  - Stuttering and cluttering are examples of fluency disorders.

C. Voice Disorders
  - Dysphonia describes any condition of _____

- A phonation disorder causes the voice to sound _____

- Resonance disorders are _____ or _____

D. Language Impairments
  - An expressive language impairment interferes with _____ of language.

  - A receptive language impairment interferes with _____ of language.

V. Identification and Assessment
  - Communication disorders are usually first identified by _____

  - Evaluation components include _____

    _____

    _____

VI. Educational Approaches
  - The speech-language pathologist is the school-based professional with the primary responsibility

    for _____

A. Treating Speech Sound Errors
  - articulation errors and phonological errors: _____

  - fluency disorders: _____

  - voice disorders: _____

  - language disorders: _____
B. Augmentative and alternative communication

  - AAC has three components: _____

    _____

VII. Educational Placement Alternatives
  - 89% of children with speech and language impairments are served in _____,

    6.5% in _____, and 4.5% in _____.
  - The following service delivery models are used within these three placements: _____

    _____

    _____

VIII. Current Issues and Future Trends
  - Specialists will probably function even more indirectly in the future.
  - SLP professionals will deal with the controversy as to whether services should take a

    _____ versus _____ focus.

- Changing populations means growing caseloads and more children with severe and multiple disabilities being served.

- "Across the day" interventions mean that interventions must be applicable not only in the classroom but by _____

In Class Activities

Response Card Activity: Identify the Type of Articulation Disorder

Articulation Disorders: substitutions, omissions, additions, distortions

1. Six-year-old Maria says "wight" for "right."

2. Five-year-old Terry says "pay" instead of "play."

3. Ten-year-old Michael says "buhrown" instead of "brown."

4. Elmer Fudd says "wascally wabbit" instead of "rascally rabbit."

5. Marsha whistles when she says the "s" sound.

6. Daniel says "cool" instead of "school."

7. Darrell says "fahlower" instead of "flower."

8. Elaine is difficult to understand because she produces frequent non-language sounds when she speaks.

9. Matthew says "garbarage" instead of "garbage."

10. Marlena says "ca" instead of "cat."

11. Donald says "telphone" instead of "telephone."

12. Myrna says "monkeny" instead of "monkey."

13. Alex says "dis" and "dat" instead of "this" and "that."

14. Paul says "screet" instead of "street."

Response Card Activity: Identify the type of Voice, Fluency, or Language Disorder

Voice, Fluency, and Language Disorders: phonation, resonance, stuttering, expressive, receptive

1. What kind of speech disorder does Porky Pig have?

2. Steven is unable to follow a sequence of simple directions.

3. Yvonne always sounds as if she has a head cold when she speaks.

4. Lewis rapidly repeats consonant and vowel sounds at the beginning of words.

5. Theresa sounds like she has a sore throat whenever she talks.

6. Georgina has difficulty understanding others when they speak to her.

7. Francine causes distress to her listeners because her voice is unusually high-pitched and strained.

8. Frank has a very limited vocabulary and usually communicates through gestures.

9.   Melissa talks through her nose which gives her voice an unpleasant twang.

10. Vera is hard to understand because her voice is too breathy.

Homework

Write a 2 page position paper on the following topic

Write a 2-page discussion paper addressing the following question: Should all children in the United States be expected to speak Standard American English regardless of their cultural, social, or geographic background? Explain why or why not.

What Do You Think?
The Role of a Speech Language Pathologist

A Speech and Language Pathologist (SLP) has been traditionally responsible for providing services to students with communication disorders, usually with "pull-out" sessions. With the enhanced emphasis on inclusion, their role appears to be changing. In the *Current Issues and Future Trends* section, Heward discusses a few of the issues related to SLP. However, SLPs are not trained teachers and hold no certification in teaching. In your paper, address the following questions: What role should an SLP take in the classroom? Should SLPs also be trained in instructional methods? How can a teacher help integrate the SLP in the classroom? See the website links below to assist you in developing your answer.

Resources and Suggestions for Exploration

American Speech-Language-Hearing Association: http://www.asha.org/

Speech Paths (online resource for SLPs): http://www.speechpaths.com

Division for Children with Communication Disorders: http://cec.sped.org/

Objectives _____

DEFINITIONS
1. List the three elements that are needed for communication to occur.
2. Describe the four functions of language.
3. Define language.
4. List and provide examples of the 5 dimensions of language.
5. Define speech.
6. Define communication disorder.
7. Compare and contrast the definitions of speech impairments and language disorders.

PREVALENCE
1. List the percentage data for students receiving special education services for speech or language impairments.

CAUSES
1. Identify the probable causes of some speech and language disorders.

CHARACTERISTICS
1. Identify and describe the types of communication disorders.

IDENTIFICATION AND ASSESSMENT
1. Describe the evaluation components for speech and language disorders.

EDUCATIONAL APPROACHES
1. Describe the treatment options for articulation, phonological, and fluency problems.
2. Define and provide examples of augmentative and alternative communication.

EDUCATIONAL PLACEMENT ALTERNATIVES
1. Describe the continuum of educational placements for students with communication disorders.

CURRENT ISSUS AND FUTURE TRENDS
1. Discuss the controversy regarding the use of speech and language pathologists in the classroom.

Self-check Quiz _____

True/False

1. The term "language learning disabilities" is used to refer to receptive and/or expressive language disorders.

2. Communication disorders represent the second largest category in special education.

3. Voice disorders involve two basic types: phonation and resonance.

4. To be eligible for special education services, a child's communication disorder must have an adverse effect on learning.

5. The most effective format for language intervention is to eliminate distracting stimuli by working in a one-to-one setting.

6. Paralinguistic codes are speech modifications (e.g., intonation, pauses) that change form and meaning of a message.

7. To identify children who may need speech-language screening requires certified speech-language pathologists, given the complexity of these disorders.

8. Articulation disorders and phonological disorders are equivalent terms to describe problems with speech.

9. The letter "s" at the end of the word "shoes" is a morpheme because it carries meaning.

10. Most normally developing children need some form of drilling or direct instruction to move from developmental forms to acceptable adult forms of speech and language.

11. Most communication that occurs involves non-speech means.

12. An adult who suffers a stroke that causes her to lose the ability to use language has aphasia.

13. Almost half of those who receive special education because of another primary disability also have a communication disorder.

14. Most languages have a logical and natural structure between a set of sounds and what they represent.

15. A person with good semantics is one who understands relationships between words such as synonyms, and knows that context changes word meanings.

Essay Questions

1. Describe characteristics, basics of treatment by clinician and teacher, and prognosis for stuttering.

2. Explain the concept of dialect and its relationship to communication disorders.

CHAPTER TEN
HEARING LOSS

Focus Questions

- **In what ways do the child who is deaf and the child who is hard of hearing differ?**

Children who are deaf may be able to perceive some sound but are unable to use their hearing to understand speech. Deaf children develop speech and language skills mainly through their sense of sight. Children who are hard-of-hearing, on the other hand, have a significant hearing loss that makes special adaptations necessary. It is possible, however, for these children to respond to speech and other auditory stimuli. Children who are hard-of-hearing develop their speech and language skills mainly through the sense of hearing.

- **How do students whose cultural identity is with the Deaf community view hearing loss?**

As discussed earlier in the text, a disability may be a handicap in one environment but not in another. There may be no condition for which this is more true than a hearing impairment. When answering this question, it may be helpful to consider another question, "Is it 'nature' that attaches enormous importance to hearing in human development and learning, or is it society?" Most people live in a world where hearing is vital to virtually every aspect of their lives. Yet, there exists a "Deaf culture" that insists it is not a disability to be hearing impaired.

- **Why can't reading simply replace speech as a means of learning and understanding English?**

Years before children learn through reading, hearing is used to acquire information and develop expressive and receptive language skills. By the time typically hearing children enter school, they have a vocabulary of over 5,000 words and have already had 100 million meaningful contacts with language. Even after children learn to read, a good deal of what they learn is acquired through auditory means. Children who learn only through reading would miss out on many critical opportunities to learn and to develop basic communication skills.

- **How do advocates of oral/aural, total communication, and bilingual-bicultural approaches to educating students who are deaf differ in philosophies and teaching methods?**

The fundamental disagreement concerns the extent to which children who are deaf should express themselves through speech and perceive the communication of others through speechreading and residual hearing. Educators who primarily utilize the oral approach emphasize the development of speech and language and view speech as essential for integration into the hearing world; they often discourage the use of sign language and other gestures. Educators who utilize a total communication approach (i.e., use of sign language, gestures, cues, fingerspelling, and other manual means used along with speech) believe this to be a more natural way of communicating. They believe that this approach enables children who are hearing impaired to more fully express themselves and understand the communication of others.

- **Why do you think American Sign Language (ASL) has not been fully accepted as the language of instruction in educational programs for deaf children?**

American Sign Language (ASL) is structured to accommodate individuals who are hearing impaired. Because ASL has its own vocabulary, syntax, and grammatical rules, it does not correspond exactly to spoken or written English. This makes precise word-for-word translations between ASL and English just as difficult as word-for-word translations between different spoken languages. Many educators fail to see that ASL is a language in its own right, not a manual communication of English.

Essential Concepts _____

- Communication is necessary in nearly every aspect of a child's day-to-day routine; its role in learning social and academic skills is critical. Disorders involving a student's articulation, voice quality, fluency, or use and understanding of language can significantly influence the student's learning. It is no wonder that speech and language disorders represents the second largest disability category in terms of the number of children served.

- Normal language development follows a relatively predictable sequence. Most children learn to use language without direct instruction by age 5. When a child's language development deviates from the norm to such an extent that he or she has serious difficulties in learning and in interpersonal relations, the child is said to have a communication disorder. Special education is needed when a communication disorder adversely affects educational performance.

- As many as 5% of school-age children have speech impairments serious enough to warrant attention. Nearly twice as many boys as girls have speech impairments. Children with articulation problems represent the largest category of speech-language impairments.

- Communication disorders that are organic are attributed to a specific physical cause. Most communication disorders, however, do not have a known physical origin. Environmental influences, such as the child's opportunity to learn speech and language, are thought to be the major causes of many communication disorders.

- There are various treatment approaches to speech and language disorders. With few exceptions, however, treatment of children with such disorders involves aspects of their environment where they need to communicate. The goal of most treatment programs is to teach children to communicate with a variety of other individuals and across a variety of circumstances.

- Augmentative and alternative communication (AAC) may be necessary in severe situations. An augmentative communication system is designed to supplement and enhance a person's communication capabilities.

Chapter Ten at a Glance

Main Topics	Key Points	Key Terms
Definitions of Hearing Loss	IDEA defines hearing impairment as a hearing loss that adversely affects educational performance.	hearing impairment
		deaf
	Children who are deaf use vision as their primary modality for learning and communication, while children who are hard of hearing are able to use their hearing to understand speech.	residual hearing
		hard of hearing
		audition
	Many people who are deaf do not view their hearing loss as a disability and consider the term *hearing impairment* inappropriate and demeaning.	auditory canal
		tympanic membrane
		ossicles
	The sense of hearing is a complex and not completely understood process.	cochlea
		decibels
	Sound is measured in decibels (intensity) and hertz (frequency).	hertz
Prevalence	About 95 of every 1000 people have a chronic hearing loss (ASHA, 2001).	
	83 out of every 1000 school-age children have an educationally significant hearing loss, and 9 out of every 1000 school-age children have severe to profound hearing loss.	
	About 25% of students who are deaf or hard of hearing have another disabling condition: LD, 9%; MR, 8%; visual problems, 4%; and EBD, 4%.	
Types and Causes of Hearing Loss	Conductive hearing loss results from abnormalities of the outer or middle ear, and sensorineural hearing loss refers to damage to the inner ear.	conductive hearing loss
		sensorineural hearing loss
		unilateral
	Hearing loss can be congenital (present at birth) or acquired (appears after birth).	bilateral
		congenital
	The child whose hearing loss is prelingual (before language is acquired) has educational needs that are very different from the child whose hearing loss is postlingual (after language is acquired).	acquired
		prelingual
		postlingual
	Congenital hearing loss is caused by genetic factors, maternal rubella, CMV, or prematurity. Acquired hearing loss is caused by otitis media, meningitis, Ménière's disease, and noise exposure.	
Characteristics of Students with Hearing Loss	Students with hearing loss are a heterogeneous group.	
	A child who is unable to hear the speech sounds of other people will not learn speech and language spontaneously. Atypical speech is common for many children with hearing impairments.	
	The academic problems of students who are deaf are largely attributable to the mismatch between their perceptual abilities and the demands of spoken and written English. The extent to which a child with hearing loss successfully interacts depends largely on others' attitudes and the child's ability to communicate in some mutually accepted way.	

Chapter Ten at a Glance

Main Topics	Key Points	Key Terms
Identification and Assessment	Auditory brain stem response and otoacoustic emission screening are used to assess infants. Pure tone audiometry is used to assess older children and adults, and speech audiometry tests detection and understanding of speech.	audiometer audiogram speech audiometry speech reception threshold
Technologies and Supports to Amplify, Provide, Enhance, or Replace Sound	Hearing aids make sounds louder but not necessarily clearer; however, modern hearing aids can differentially amplify frequencies. Group assistive listening devices can solve problems caused by distance, noise, and reverberation in the classroom by establishing a radio link between the teacher and student with hearing loss. Surgically placed cochlear implants stimulate the auditory nerve directly. Many members of the Deaf community are vehemently against cochlear implants. Supports and technologies that replace sound include: interpreters, speech-to-text translation, television captioning, text telephones, and alerting devices.	cochlear implants
Educational Approaches	Oral/aural approaches, which are difficult and time consuming, focus on developing the ability to speak intelligibly. These approaches include auditory learning, speech reading, and cued speech. Total communication, the most widely used method of instruction in schools for the deaf, combines speech and manual communication (manually coded English, fingerspelling). The bilingual/bicultural approach focuses on students mastering their first language (American Sign Language) which will enable them to master reading and writing in their second language (English).	auditory learning speech reading cued speech manually coded English fingerspelling bilingual/bicultural American Sign Language
Educational Placement Alternatives	Parents have the option of choosing between their local public school or residential school placement (82% attend local public schools). Professional and parent organizations are strongly in favor of maintaining the continuum of placement options. A growing number of postsecondary educational opportunities are available to students with hearing loss.	continuum of placement options
Current Issues and Future Trends	The bilingual/bicultural approach will probably continue to be used with children served in special schools or self-contained classrooms. Many leaders of the Deaf culture do not view deafness as a disability and oppose efforts to "cure" it. Children with hearing loss should have access to the communication modality best suited for their individual needs.	

Guided Review

I. Defining Hearing Loss
- Hearing impairment indicates a hearing loss that adversely affects _____

- A child who is deaf uses _____ as the primary modality for learning and communication.

- A deaf person may perceive some sounds through _____

- Children who are hard of hearing are able to use their hearing to _____

- Many persons who are deaf do not view hearing loss as a disability.

A. How We Hear
- Audition, the sense of hearing, is a complex and not completely understood process.

- The auricle funnels sound waves into the _____

- Variations in sound pressure cause the eardrum to _____

- The vibrations of the bones of the middle ear transmit energy to the _____
- The inner ear is the most critical and complex part of the hearing apparatus.

B. The Nature of Sound
- The intensity or loudness of sound is measured in _____

- The frequency, or pitch, of sound is measured in cycles per second or _____

II. Prevalence
- According to ASHA, 95 out of _____ people have a chronic hearing loss.

- The large majority of persons with hearing loss are _____

- The U.S. Public Health Service estimates 83 out of 1000 children have _____ hearing loss.

- About 25% of students who are deaf or hard of hearing have another _____

III. Types and Causes of Hearing Loss
- Conductive hearing loss results from abnormalities of the _____

- Sensorineural hearing loss refers to damage to the _____
- Unilateral hearing loss is present in one ear, and bilateral hearing loss is present in both ears.

- Congenital hearing loss is present _____, and acquired hearing loss appears _____

- Prelingual hearing loss and postlingual hearing loss identify whether a hearing loss occurred before or after the development of spoken language.

A. Causes of Congenital Hearing Loss
   1. Genetic Factors
   2. Maternal Rubella
   3. Congenital Cytomegalovirus (CMV)
   4. Premature birth

B. Causes of Acquired Hearing Loss
   1. Otitis Media
   2. Meningitis
   3. Ménière's Disease
   4. Noise Exposure

IV. Characteristics of Students with Hearing Loss
   • Students with hearing loss comprise an extremely _____
   • Levels of functioning are influenced by degree of hearing loss, attitudes of parents and siblings,

     opportunities to _____, and the presence or absence of _____

   A. English Literacy
      • A child who is unable to hear the _____ of other people will not learn
        speech and language spontaneously.
      • Students with hearing loss have smaller vocabularies and difficulty with word function, multiple
        meaning words, and differentiating questions from statements.

      • Many deaf students write sentences that are _____

   B. Speaking
      • Atypical speech is common in many children who are deaf or hard of hearing.

   C. Academic Achievement
      • Most children with hearing loss have difficulty with _____

      • Deafness itself imposes no limitations on the _____

   D. Social Functioning
      • The extent to which a child with hearing loss successfully interacts depends largely on others'

        _____ and the child's ability to communicate in some _____

V. Identification and Assessment
   A. Assessment of Infants
      • The two most widely used methods of screening for hearing loss include measuring
        physiological reactions to sound.
      • auditory brain stem response: _____

      • otoacoustic emission screening: _____

   C. Pure-Tone Audiometry
      • The examiner uses an _____ to assess hearing. The results are plotted on a

        chart called an _____

   D. Speech Audiometry
      • Speech audiometry tests a person's _____ of speech to
        determine the speech reception threshold.

E. Alternative Audiometric Techniques
- Play audiometry: _____

- Operant conditioning audiometry: _____

- Behavior observation audiometry: _____

F. Degrees of Hearing Loss
- Hearing loss is usually described by the terms _____

VI. Technologies and Supports to Amplify, Provide, Enhance, or Replace Sound.
A. Hearing Aids
- Modern hearing aids can differentially _____

- Hearing aids make sounds louder but _____

- The earlier in life a child can be _____, the more effectively he will learn to use hearing for communication and awareness.

- Hearing aids offer minimal benefit in _____

B. Assistive Listening Devices
- A radio link established between the teacher and the child can solve problems caused by

_____

C. Cochlear Implants
- A cochlear implant bypasses damaged hair cells and _____

- Tremendous controversy surrounds cochlear implants in the _____

D. Supports and Technologies
1. Interpreters
2. Speech-to-Text Translation
3. Television Captioning
4. Text Telephones
5. Alerting Devices

VII. Educational Approaches _____
A. Oral/Aural Approaches
- Training in producing and understanding speech is _____

_____

- Oral emphasis programs typically use several means to develop _____
- The oral approach is difficult, demanding, and time consuming.
- The best results are for children who are integrated most of the day into _____
1. Auditory Learning _____
2. Speechreading
3. Cued Speech

B. Total Communication
    • Simultaneous presentation of language by speech and manual communication.

    • Total communication has become the most _____ in
    • schools for the deaf
    1. Manually Coded English
    2. Fingerspelling

C. American Sign Language (ASL) and the Bilingual-Bicultural Approach

    • ASL is the language of the Deaf culture in the _____

    • ASL is a legitimate language _____

    • ASL does not correspond to _____

    • The goal of the bilingual-bicultural education approach is to help deaf students become

    _____

    _____

VIII. Educational Placement Alternatives
    • Approximately 82% of children who are deaf or hard of hearing attend _____
    • While full inclusion in regular classrooms has benefited some deaf students, all of the professional
      and parent organizations involved with educating students who are deaf have issued position

      statements strongly in favor of _____

A. Postsecondary Education
    • The percentage of students with hearing loss who attend postsecondary educational programs
      has risen dramatically in the past 20 years.
    • About _____ of all students with hearing loss go on to receive higher education.

IX. Current Issues and Future Trends
    • Given the large percentage of children with hearing loss who are educated in regular classrooms

      for most of the day, it is likely that _____ and _____ methods of
      instruction will continue to be used.

    • The _____ approach will probably be used with a growing percentage of the
      deaf students served in special schools and self-contained classrooms.

    • Many leaders of the _____ do not view deafness as a disability and oppose efforts
      to "cure" it.

    • The keys to improving the future for people who are deaf or hard of hearing are access to the
      language and communication modality best suited to individual needs and preferences, effective
      instruction with meaningful curriculum, and self-advocacy.

In Class Activities

Response Card Activity: Identify types of hearing loss

Identify the following as: congenital, adventitious, unilateral, bilateral, conductive, or sensorineural.

1. This hearing loss is prelingual.

2. This hearing impairment is acquired after birth.

3. This hearing impairment is present at birth.

4. When children have this hearing impairment, teachers must focus on acquisition of speech.

5. When children have this hearing impairment, teachers must focus on maintenance of speech.

6. This hearing loss is postlingual.

7. This hearing impairment is present in only one ear.

8. This hearing impairment is present in both ears.

9. This hearing impairment is caused by damage to the inner ear.

10. A hearing aid is more effective with this type of hearing loss.

11. With this hearing impairment, sound is delivered to the brain in a distorted fashion or not at all.

12. This hearing impairment is caused by damage to the middle or outer ear.

13. This hearing impairment can often be corrected with surgery.

14. This hearing loss refers to damage of the auditory nerve fibers.

15. A buildup of excessive wax in the auditory canal can cause this type of hearing loss.

16. This hearing loss can be caused if eardrum ossicles do not move properly.

Response Card Activity: Levels of auditory training

Identify the following levels of auditory training as: awareness, localization, discrimination, or comprehension.

1. In this level of auditory training, children are trained to detect the presence of sound.

2. In this level of auditory training, children are taught to identify the meaning of sounds.

3. In this level of auditory training, children are taught to distinguish between sounds.

4. In this level of auditory training, children are taught to find the direction from which the sound is coming.

5. Jeremy can tell the difference between a high-pitched sound and a low-pitched sound.

6. Brian can understand a short list of directions.

7. Donald can tell if the dog is barking.

8. Sylvia can distinguish the difference between the words "cat" and "cake."

9. Eugene can tell if the phone is ringing.

10. Olivia can recognize a voice on the telephone.

11. Eula can tell where the siren is coming from.

12. Harvey can understand a message on the intercom.

Homework

After reading the PROFILES & PERSPECTIVES features, "Defiantly Deaf: Deaf People Live, Proudly, in Another Culture, but Not a Lesser One" and "Deafness: The Dilemma," write a 2-3 page paper explaining your perspective on the extent to which deafness is a culture and to what extent deafness is a disability.

What Do You Think?
Modes and Languages of Communication: Supports or Barriers for Students Who Are Deaf or Hard of Hearing?

At the El Paso Regional Day Program, we use a SEE/Total Communication approach. SEE (Signing Exact English) is not a language. It's a way to encode English so that students will develop a stronger command of the language. Some educators argue that because ASL is the true native language of American Deaf people, giving students a strong base in ASL will make it easier for them to acquire English as a second language. There are also advocates of programs that use other types of communication in the classroom such as manually coded English, cued speech, and oralism (though there are fewer purely oral programs these days).

Deaf education is a field with many knock-down, drag-out controversies, and most of them center around communication. To say that this is an area of some controversy is to say that many people got their hair mussed during the course of World War 2. - Douglas Jackson

The education of children who are deaf or hard of hearing is one of the most challenging, complex, and interesting areas in all of special education. It is extremely difficult to teach an orally based language to children with limited ability to hear. It should not come as a surprise, then, that many methods for teaching the deaf have been developed and tried, most with limited, although some, success. Most research and debate in deaf education today focuses on which language and mode of communication should be used in the classroom.

The Assignment

Select a particular approach or method of instruction used in deaf education. Explore and learn about that method using one or more of the resources below as a starting point for your research. Write a position paper outlining your perspectives and recommendations concerning the approach or method with respect to this question: *How might the language and mode of instruction used to teach students who are deaf (or Deaf) support or impede their acquisition of English literacy skills, academic achievement, social functioning, and/or self-concept?*

Related Issues to Consider
- What are the functions of classroom communication?
- How does the setting in which a deaf student is educated impact the mode of communication?

Resources and Suggestions for Exploration
> The Internet is teeming with sites dealing with deafness. I think that the computer has done more to bring deaf people in touch with each other than any other development of the 20th century.
> - Douglas Jackson

Laurent Clerc National Deaf Education Center, Gallaudet University: http://clerccenter.gallaudet.edu/

ERIC Documents on Instructional Approaches: http://ericec.org/

Oral Approach: http://www.agbell.org/

Cued Speech: http://www.cuedspeech.com/home.cfm

Signing Exact English: http://www.seecenter.org/

Cochlear Implants: http://www.odysseyweekly.com/052001/soundandfury/

National Association of the Deaf: http://www.nad.org/

Objectives

DEFINITIONS
1. List the 3 elements that that are needed for communication to occur.
2. Describe the 4 functions of language.
3. Define language.
4. List and provide examples of the 5 dimensions of language.
5. Define speech.
6. Define communication disorder.
7. Compare and contrast the definitions of speech impairments and language disorders.

PREVALENCE
1. List the percentage data for students receiving special education services for speech or language impairments.

CAUSES
1. Identify the probable causes of some speech and language disorders.

CHARACTERISTICS
1. Identify and describe the types of communication disorders.

IDENTIFICATION AND ASSESSMENT
1. Describe the evaluation components for speech and language disorders.

EDUCATIONAL APPROACHES
1. Describe the treatment options for articulation, phonological, and fluency problems.
2. Define and provide examples of augmentative and alternative communication.

EDUCATIONAL PLACEMENT ALTERNATIVES
1. Describe the continuum of educational placements for students with communication disorders.

CURRENT ISSUES AND FUTURE TRENDS
1. Discuss the controversy regarding the use of speech and language pathologists in the classroom.

Self-check Quiz

True/False

1. Most students with a hearing impairment are educated in the public schools.

2. A person who can hear sounds of a frequency between 500 and 5000 Hz can hear men's voices more easily than women's.

3. Most students who are deaf or hard of hearing also have another disabling condition, such as learning disabilities.

4. A conductive hearing loss originates in the outer or middle ear.

5. Noise exposure is the leading cause of postlingual hearing loss.

6. The main receptor organ for hearing is the tympanic membrane.

7. For the hearing impaired, the development of language and communication skills is the primary objective of all instructional approaches.

8. Nearly all deaf children have some amount of residual hearing.

9. ASL is a visual-spatial form of English.

10. Children with hearing impairments are more likely than their hearing peers to have social and emotional difficulties.

11. Hearing aids work by amplifying all sounds, to enable better use of residual hearing.

12. The bilingual/bicultural approach prioritizes the learning of ASL over English.

13. Deaf infants do not babble, coo, or smile like hearing infants.

14. IDEA '97 requires that the communication needs of a student who is deaf be considered on the IEP.

Essay Questions

1. Distinguish between the terms "deaf" and "Deaf."

2. Compare and contrast different forms of audiometry.

CHAPTER ELEVEN
BLINDNESS AND LOW VISION

*Focus Questions*_____

- **In what ways does loss of vision affect learning?**

Consider all the events in the environment that are perceived through vision. Hearing, taste, touch, and smell help to add detail to what is seen, but it is vision that plays the critical role in learning to interact with the various features of the environment. Sighted individuals may take for granted all of the information obtained through the eyes and the relative ease with which this visual information is learned. It is not difficult to make a list of the academic skills that children with visual impairments will have difficulty learning because of the absence or distortion of visual information. But learning is not limited to academics. Knowing when a classmate or teacher is disappointed or pleased, eating without embarrassment in the school cafeteria, and interacting appropriately in social situations are also largely dependent on visual information. Special instructional methods and equipment are often necessary for children with visual impairments to help them acquire the academic and social skills necessary for independent and productive living.

- **How does the age at which vision is lost affect the student?**

One factor that influences instructional decisions for children with visual impairments is the point in the child's life when the vision loss occurred. Congenital visual impairments are present at birth. Adventitious visual impairment is acquired at some point during a person's life. A child who is adventitiously blind usually retains some visual memory, and the teacher can take advantage of the images the child recalls when designing teaching programs and instructional activities. Teaching the words "dog" and "blue" will be much easier if the child has seen a dog or things that are blue. Children with a congenital visual impairment, however, have no visual history and will often require education programming that makes use of their nonvisual experiences. Learning what dogs are can be accomplished through the sense of touch, but touching dogs is not the same as seeing dogs. Concepts such as blueness, as simple as they are for most normally sighted children to learn, may be impossible for children with congenital visual impairments to understand. Additionally, the level of emotional support and acceptance will differ for children who are adventitiously blind and congenitally blind. The child who must make a sudden adjustment to the loss of vision will probably require a great deal of emotional support.

- **Normally sighted children enter school with a great deal of knowledge about trees. How could a teacher help the young child who is congenitally blind develop the concept of trees?**

Because the visual impairment has been present since birth, the child has a total absence of visual memory. Verbal descriptions of the tree may add something to the child's understanding, but the teaching approach will have to rely primarily on direct, firsthand contact with trees through the child's other senses. This design of the teaching program must allow the child to experience a wide range of tactile, olfactory, auditory, and other sensory stimuli, all of which add to the essence of a tree and help convey that trees are of different sizes, shapes, and types. This teaching approach for the concept of a tree will be similar to the teaching approach for the many other concepts that students with visual impairments must learn.

- **What compensatory skills do students with visual impairments need most?**

A basic goal of special education concerns teaching skills for independent and productive living. Academic skills alone will not accomplish this goal. Learning life skills such as cooking, grooming, managing money, participating in leisure activities, and coping with societal expectations are essential parts of any curriculum for exceptional learners. In addition, children with visual impairments should know how to explain their disability to others and to refrain from behaviors such as rocking and head rolling that draw undue, and often negative, attention to their disabilities. Because most students with visual impairments are educated in regular school settings, it is easy to focus attention exclusively on academic skills. It is important to recognize, however, that academics are but one part of a curriculum necessary to prepare students with visual impairment for life beyond the classroom.

- **How do the educational goals and instructional methods for children with low vision differ from those of children who are blind?**

As do children in all other categories of exceptionality, children with visual impairments exhibit a wide range of abilities. Children who are identified as blind generally have little or no useful vision. Children with low vision, on the other hand, often have residual vision so that with various types of ocular aids, such as large print or magnifiers, they can use printed materials in their classrooms and communities. Children with visual impairments have different levels of visual ability, but the goal of instruction is the same for all these children: to teach them skills that will enable them to take their place in society as productive, self-sufficient individuals.

Essential Concepts

- The legal definition of blindness is based on a person's ability to see clearly at specified distances as well as a person's peripheral vision. The educational definition focuses on the effects of visual impairment on the child's academic performance.

- Children with visual impairment display a wide range of visual capabilities, from blindness-the total absence of useful vision-to low vision-which can be quite useful for learning. All of these students, however, require special educational modifications to assist their progress in regular educational programs.

- The age of onset of a visual impairment is an important consideration in programming. Children who have been blind from birth have no visual history to apply to their current learning needs. Adventitiously blind children, on the other hand, have had some visual experiences, which typically facilitate the teaching of many skills.

- By using Braille and a host of manipulative, technological, and optical aids, children with visual impairment can participate in academic programs with their normally sighted peers. Academics cannot, however, be the exclusive focus of educational programs. Gaining social skills, meeting expectations, finding suitable work, exploring sexuality, and other basic life experiences are as important as academics. In addition, specialized training in orientation and mobility is essential to ensuring the independence of students who are blind or have low vision.

Chapter Eleven at a Glance

Main Topics	Key Points	Key Terms
Definitions of Visual Impairment	Legal blindness is defined by having visual acuity of 20/200 or less in the better eye after the best possible correction, and/or a field of vision of less than 20 degrees. Educational definitions of totally blind, functionally blind, and low vision focus on the extent to which students are able to use the visual channel for learning. Age of onset (whether the visual impairment is present at birth or acquired later) is an important factor for determining educational programming and support.	visual acuity field of vision legally blind totally blind functionally blind low vision congenital adventitious
Prevalence	Children with visual impairments constitute a very small percentage of the school-age population (fewer than 2 children in 1000).	
Types and Causes of Visual Impairment	Effective vision requires proper functioning of the optical system, the muscular system, and the nervous system. Causes of visual impairment are grouped into three categories: refractive errors (e.g., myopia, hyperopia); structural impairments (e.g., cataracts, glaucoma, nystagmus, strabismus); and cortical visual impairments.	cornea lens vitreous humor retina ocular motility optic nerve
Characteristics of Students with Visual Impairments	Children with visual impairments need explicit experience with the environment in order to organize and make connections between experiences. Abstract concepts can be particularly difficult for children who cannot see. Children with low vision have poorer motor skills than sighted children. Some students with visual impairment experience problems with social adjustment and interaction due to limited common experiences with sighted peers; inability to see and use eye contact, facial expressions, and gestures during conversations; and/or stereotypic behavior. The attitudes and behavior of sighted persons may present unnecessary barriers for social participation of students with low vision.	incidental learning stereotypic behavior
Educational Approaches	Special adaptations for students who are blind include the use of braille for reading and writing; tactile aids and manipulatives (e.g., Cranmer abacus, Speech-Plus talking calculator, embossed relief maps and diagrams); technological aids for reading print (e.g., Optacon, Kurzweil reading system); and assistive computer technology (e.g., magnifying screen images, speech recognition, and conversion of text files into synthesized speech).	braille MAVIS SAVI Optacon

Chapter Eleven at a Glance

Main Topics	Key Points	Key Terms
Educational Approaches (continued)	Functional vision cannot be determined by measures of visual acuity and field of vision. Systematic training can help students use their limited vision more effectively.	functional vision orientation mobility laser beam cane Mowat sensor SonicGuide
	Special adaptations for students with low vision include optical devices (e.g., glasses, contacts, small hand-held telescopes, magnifiers); large print text; and a variety of classroom adaptations such as desk lamps, desks with tilting tops, and off-white writing paper.	
	Training in orientation (knowing your location) and mobility (moving safely from one point to another) is necessary for increasing independent functioning for people with visual impairments.	
	Orientation and mobility aids include the long cane, guide dogs, sighted guides, and electronic travel aids.	
	Children with low vision do not develop important listening skills automatically. They need specific instruction in becoming aware of sounds, discriminating differences between sounds, identifying the sources of sounds, and attaching meaning to sounds.	
	Curriculum goals for students with visual impairments should include functional living skills (e.g., cooking, shopping, transportation).	
Educational Placement Alternatives	About 90% of students with visual impairments attend local public schools.	
	In many districts, a specially trained itinerant vision specialist provides support to students with low vision and their regular classroom teachers.	
	The current population of residential schools consists largely of children with visual impairments with additional disabilities, such as mental retardation, hearing impairment, behavioral disorders, and cerebral palsy.	
	Most parents can choose between public day and residential schools for their children with visual impairments.	
Current Issues and Future Trends	Children with visual impairments are likely to receive special education services in the future in both regular and residential schools.	
	Career opportunities will likely expand as individuals with visual impairments become more aware of their legal and human rights.	

Guided Review _____

I. Definitions of Visual Impairment
   A. Legal Definition of Blindness
      - The legal definition is based on _____ and _____
      - A person whose visual acuity is 20/200 or less after the best possible correction with glasses

        or contact lenses is considered _____

      - A person whose vision is restricted to an area of _____ is considered
        legally blind.

   B. Educational Definitions of Visual Impairments
      The IDEA definition emphasizes the relationship between _____

      - totally blind: _____

      - functionally blind: _____

      - low vision: _____

   C. Age of Onset
      - Visual impairment can be _____ (present at birth) or _____ (acquired).
      - The age of onset has implications for how children with low vision should be taught.

II. Prevalence
   - Fewer than 2 children in 1000 have visual impairments.
   - Almost half of school age children with visual impairments have at least _____

III. Types and Causes of Visual Impairment
   A. How We See
      - Effective vision requires proper functioning of three anatomical systems: _____

        _____

      - The eye's optical system collects and focuses light energy reflected from objects in the visual
        field.

      - Six muscles attached to the outside of each eye enable it to _____

        _____

      - Inside the eye, tiny muscles adjust the shape of the lens in order to focus.
      - The eye's nervous system converts light energy into electrical impulses and transmits that
        information to the brain where it is processed into visual images.

   B. Causes of Visual Impairments
      1. Refractive errors: _____

      2. Structural impairments: _____

      3. Cortical visual impairments: _____

        _____

IV. Characteristics of Students with Visual Impairments
   A. Cognition and Language
      • Impaired or absent vision makes it difficult to see the connections between experiences.

   B. Motor Development and Mobility
      • Visual impairment often leads to delays and deficits in motor development.

   C. Social Adjustment and Interaction
      • Children with visual impairments interact less and are often delayed in _____

      • Some individuals with visual impairments engage in _____ behavior.
      • Many persons who have lost their sight report that the biggest difficulty socially is dealing

         with _____

V. Educational Approaches
   A. Special Adaptations for Students Who are Blind_____

     1. Braille is a tactile system of _____

        _____

     2. Braille Technological Aids have made Braille more efficient, thus enabling many students to

        _____

     3. Declining Braille Literacy
        • In response to the concern over declining Braille literacy, the 1997 amendments to IDEA

           specified that IEP teams _____

           _____

     4. Tactile Aids and Manipulatives
        Mathematical aids: _____

        Science and Social Studies Aids: _____

        _____

     5. Technological Aids for Reading Print include: _____
     6. Computer Access
        Assistive technologies include: _____

        _____

   B. Special Adaptations for Students with Low Vision
     1. Functional Vision
        • The fundamental premise underlying the development of functional vision is that

           _____

           _____

     2. Optical Devices include: _____
     3. Reading Print
        • Students with low vision use three basic approaches for reading print: _____

           _____

- In addition to print size, other equally important factors to consider are: _____

_____

4. Classroom Adaptations include: _____

_____

C. Expanded Curriculum Priorities
   1. Orientation and Mobility (O&M)

      - Orientation is _____

      - Mobility involves _____

      - O&M is considered a _____ by IDEA.
   2. Cane Skills
      - The long cane is the most widely used device for adults with severe visual impairments

        who _____
      - Properly used, the cane serves as both a _____
   3. Guide Dogs
      - Less than _____ of people with visual impairments travel with the aid of guide dogs.
   4. Sighted Guides
   5. Electronic travel aids include: _____
   6. Listening Skills
      - A widely held misconception is that persons who are blind automatically _____

        _____

      - The systematic development of listening skills is an important component of the

        _____

      - Listening involves _____

        _____

   7. Functional Life Skills
      - Specific instruction and ongoing supports should be provided to ensure that students with

        visual impairments learn skills such as _____

        _____

VI. Educational Placement Alternatives
   - 90% of children with visual impairments are educated in public schools.
   A. Itinerant Teacher Model
      - Most students who are included in general education classrooms receive support from

        _____

      - Some public schools have special resource rooms for students with visual impairments.

      - The most important factor to the successful inclusion of students with visual impairments is

        the regular classroom teacher's _____

- Other aspects of the school situation found to be highly important were _____

  _____

  _____

B. Residential Schools
  - About _____ of school-age children with visual impairments attend residential schools.
  - The current population of residential schools consists largely of children with visual

    impairments with additional disabilities, such as _____

    _____

  - Advantages of residential schools include _____

    _____

    _____

VII. Current Issues and Future Trends
  A. Specialization of Services
     - Children with visual impairments are likely to receive special education services in the future in both regular and residential schools.
     - Greater emphasis will be placed on intervention with infants and young children and on training older students for independence.
  B. Emerging Technology and Research
     - It is hoped that all people with visual impairments will benefit from new technological and biomedical developments.
     - Artificial sight may be possible in the future.
  C. Fighting Against Discrimination and for Self-determination
     - Career opportunities will likely expand as individuals with visual impairments become more aware of their legal and human rights.

In Class Activities

Pair up with another student. One of you will wear a blindfold, and the other will be the sighted guide. Go to a safe area of campus (i.e., free of motorized traffic). The sighted guide will spin the blindfolded student around five times (slowly) and then act as a guide to get him/her back to the classroom. The sighted guide is not allowed to tell the student where he/she is in relation to the class but only to provide safety instructions (e.g., "you need to step up here, there are some steps"). After you have made it back to the classroom, respond to the following questions: (a) What methods did you use to help get you back to the classroom? (b) What other senses did you rely on as you navigated your way back to class? (c) What sorts of feelings did you have during this activity?

Small Group Activity: Identify the most important functional skills for students with visual impairments

The TEACHING & LEARNING feature, "I Made It Myself, and It's Good!" describes a study in which blind students use a Walkman to learn how to cook. Brainstorm with your small group to compile a list of other functional skills that should receive priority when selecting instructional objectives for students who are blind. Sequence the critical skills from most important to least important. Share your group's list during large group discussion.

Homework

Write a 2 page position paper on one of the following topics

1. Which child do you think would be more difficult to teach, the child with congenital blindness or the child with acquired blindness? Explain why.

2. It has been suggested that children with visual impairments are the easiest group of students with disabilities to integrate into the regular classroom. Would you agree or disagree with this statement? Explain.

3. Under what circumstances (if any) do you think a student with a visual impairment should attend a residential school?

What Do You Think?
People with Visual Impairments and Employment

Many people tend to underestimate the capacity of individuals with visual impairments. Consequently, people with visual impairments have been denied the full range of occupational and personal choices. Write a 4-5 page paper that responds to the following: What do you think the biggest hurdles are for people with visual impairments in obtaining and maintaining employment? Identify solutions to the problems of barriers to employment and meeting the specific needs of unemployed people with visual impairments.

Resources and Suggestions for Exploration

Hutto, M. D., & Thompson, A. R. (1995). Career advancement for young women with visual impairments. Journal of Visual Impairment and Blindness, 91, 280-296.

Hutto, M. D., & Thompson, A. R. (1995). Counseling college students with visual impairments in preparation for employment. Re:View, 27, 29-36.

Nagle, K. M. (2001). Transition to employment and community life for youths with visual impairments: Current status and future directions. Journal of Visual Impairment and Blindness, 95, 725-739.

O'Day, B. (1999). Employment barriers for people with visual impairments. <u>Journal of Visual Impairment and Blindness, 93,</u> 459-462.

Wolffe, K. (1998). Preparing people with visual impairments for work. <u>Journal of Visual Impairment and Blindness, 2,</u> 111-115.

Wolffe, K. (1999). Responding to a common concern about hiring people with visual impairments: Access to print information. <u>Journal of Visual Impairment and Blindness, 93,</u> 110-114.

Young, C. E. (1999). Turning negatives into positives at job interviews for people who are visually impaired. <u>Journal of Visual Impairment and Blindness, 93,</u> 459-462.

Objectives

DEFINITIONS OF VISUAL IMPAIRMENTS
1. List the legal definition of blindness.
2. Define visual acuity and describe what is meant by "normal vision."
3. List the educational definition of visual impairment.
4. Discuss why age of onset is an important concern for special educators.

PREVALENCE
1. List the prevalence figures for children with visual impairments.

TYPES AND CAUSES OF VISUAL IMPAIRMENTS
1. Describe how a person sees.
2. Define and describe the causes of visual impairments.

CHARACTERISTICS OF STUDENTS WITH VISUAL IMPAIRMENTS
1. Discuss how vision affects other areas of development.

EDUCATIONAL APPROACHES
1. Discuss the types of technological assistance available to students who are blind.
2. Discuss the types of technological assistance available to students with low vision.
3. Define and describe orientation and mobility training.

EDUCATIONAL PLACEMENT ALTERNATIVES
1. Describe the continuum of educational placements for students with visual impairments.

CURRENT ISSUES AND FUTURE TRENDS
1. Discuss the issues facing the future of the education of students with visual impairments.

Self-check Quiz

True/False

1. Some students with visual impairments can learn to totally compensate for their vision loss by making use of their other senses.

2. In myopia, the eye is longer than normal, causing the image to fall in front of the retina.

3. Of visually impaired children in grades K through 12, three times as many read visually than read via Braille.

4. Unlike other disabilities covered by IDEA, visual impairment has both legal and educational definitions.

5. By definition, a visual impairment requires that something be wrong with your eyes.

6. Stereotypical behaviors are seen in virtually all students with visual impairments at some point during their development.

7. 90% of children with visual impairments are educated in public schools, with over half of them educated in regular classrooms at least part of the day.

8. As a general rule of thumb, when finding print reading materials for a visually impaired child capable of reading, the larger the print size, the better.

9.   Zach is not considered legally blind because, with glasses, his visual acuity improves from 20/200 to 20/100.

10. Regarding classroom adaptations, the most effective low-vision device is proper light.

11. By default, a child who meets the federal definition of legally blind qualifies for special education.

12. Most children with visual impairments develop an increased sense of hearing to compensate for their loss of visual information.

13. Visual impairments in children preclude most incidental learning.

14. A child with low vision uses vision as a primary means of learning.

15. A person with "20/20 vision" has perfect vision.

Essay Questions

1.   As they develop curriculum and plan instruction, describe the basic premises a teacher should have about low vision and its effects on a person.

2.   Describe the expanded core curriculum for students with visual impairments, and give an example for each as might be provided to Tony, a 12-year-old student who became totally blind after a recent auto accident.

CHAPTER TWELVE
PHYSICAL DISABILITIES, HEALTH IMPAIRMENTS, AND TRAUMATIC BRAIN INJURY

*Focus Questions*_____

- **In what ways might the visibility of a physical disability or health impairment affect a child's self-perception, social development, and level of independence across different environments?**

  Earlier in the text the relative nature of disabilities was discussed-a disability might lead to educational, personal, or social problems in one setting, while in another setting may not be handicapping at all. Although this is true for all disabilities, it may be more obvious for the child with a physical or health disability. For example, a child with an artificial limb may be handicapped when competing against nondisabled peers on the baseball field, but experience no handicap in the classroom. Also, students with physical disabilities will have different learning experiences in different environments depending upon how individuals in those environments act towards them. For example, students with physical disabilities are likely to have markedly different and perhaps more challenging outdoor experiences in a camp setting where counselors are comfortable working with them than in a camp setting where counselors are overly concerned about their physical or health disabilities.

- **How do the nature and severity of a child's physical disability affect IEP goals and objectives?**

  When a child with physical disabilities needs special education, an IEP is developed. Students with physical disabilities may require modifications to the physical environment, teaching techniques, or other aspects of their educational programs. Some children with physical disabilities are extremely restricted in their activities, whereas others have few limitations on what they can do or learn. The goals and objectives of the IEP must match the individual needs of the child with physical disabilities. Modifications in the learning environment, including both physical and instructional adaptations, must be reflected in the IEP.

- **What are some of the problems that members of transdisciplinary teams for students with severe physical disabilities and multiple health needs must guard against?**

  Members of transdisciplinary teams must guard against anything that interferes with open communication with one another. No other group of exceptional children comes into contact, both in and out of school, with as many different teachers, physicians, therapists, and other specialists. Because the medical, educational, therapeutic, vocational, and social needs of students with physical and health impairments are often complex and frequently affect each other, it is especially important that educational and health care personnel openly communicate and cooperate with one another.

- **How might an assistive technology device be a hindrance as well as a help?**

  Special devices or adaptations often are necessary for children with physical or health impairments to function successfully. There is, however, an unfortunate side effect to them: their use makes the disability more conspicuous. The more conspicuous the disability, the more inclined others might be to react to the disability first and to the child as a person second. All children need to develop positive views of themselves, and inappropriate reactions from parents, teachers, classmates, and others have a decidedly negative impact on a child's self-esteem.

- **Of the many ways in which the classroom environment and instruction can be modified to support the inclusion of students with physical and health impairments, and traumatic brain injury, which are most important?**

  Teachers of children with physical and health impairments frequently find it necessary to adapt equipment, schedules, or settings so that their students can participate more fully in educational and recreational activities. Although there is currently an increasing trend toward integrating children with physical and health problems, this practice has raised several controversial issues. These issues revolve around determining the extent to which teachers and schools should realistically be expected to care for students with physical and health-related disabilities. Decisions concerning the safety for all students must be made. Perhaps the most important classroom modification is creating an atmosphere in which the student with disabilities feels socially accepted and comfortable enough to learn and contribute.

Essential Concepts

- This chapter describes a population of individuals who are more different than alike. On one end of the spectrum are children with health problems but almost no physical limitations, such as those with asthma, hemophilia, or seizure disorders. On the other end are children with physical impairments such as cerebral palsy, spina bifida, or muscular dystrophy. Many students with physical or health impairments do not have cognitive impairments and can learn at the same rate as their non-disabled peers given the right accommodations and modifications. For no other group of exceptional learners is the continuum of educational services more relevant.

- The actual number of children with physical impairments and other health impairments is much higher than those receiving services in those categories. Many children are served under other categories. In addition, in order to qualify for special education services, the child's disability must adversely affect his or her educational performance.

- The three variables that are critically important to a child's development are the age at which the disability was acquired (prenatal, perinatal, or postnatal), the severity with which the condition affects different areas of functioning, and the visibility of the impairment.

- Educational approaches for these children often involve the collaboration of an interdisciplinary team of teachers, physical and occupational therapists, speech therapists, and other health care specialists. Children with physical disabilities may also need environmental modifications such as wheelchair-accessible classrooms or other assistive technology.

- How others react to a child with physical disabilities or health impairments is at least as important as the disability itself. In all cases it is important for teachers, classmates, and the general public to have an inclusive attitude toward this group of exceptional learners.

Chapter Twelve at a Glance

Main Topics	Key Points	Key Terms
Physical Disabilities and Health Impairments	Children with physical disabilities and health impairments are eligible for special education under two disability categories: orthopedic impairments and other health impairments.	orthopedic impairment neuromotor impairment chronic conditions acute conditions
	Orthopedic impairments involve the skeletal system, and neuromotor impairments involve the nervous system.	cerebral palsy prenatal postnatal perinatal
	Physical disabilities and health impairments may be congenital or acquired, chronic or acute.	monoplegia hemiplegia triplegia
	According to IDEA, a child is entitled to special education services if his or her educational performance is adversely affected by a physical disability or health-related condition.	quadriplegia paraplegia diplegia
	Children receiving special education services under the disability category of orthopedic impairments and other health impairments represent a little less than 5% of all school-age children.	double hemiplegia spastic cerebral palsy athetoid cerebral palsy
	Cerebral palsy is a permanent condition resulting from a lesion to the brain or abnormality of brain growth.	ataxic cerebral palsy hypotonia spina bifida
	Spina bifida is a congenital condition in which the vertebrae do not enclose the spinal cord. Types of spina bifida include: spina bifida occulta, meningocele, and myelomeningocele.	spina bifida occulta meningocele myelomeningocele
	Muscular dystrophy refers to a group of inherited diseases marked by progressive atrophy of the body's muscles.	hydrocephalus shunt
	Spinal cord injuries usually result in some form of paralysis below the site of the injury.	muscular dystrophy epilepsy
	Epilepsy is characterized by various types of chronic and frequent seizures.	generalized tonic clonic seizure absence seizure
	Diabetes is a chronic disorder of metabolism.	complex partial seizure simple partial seizure
	Asthma, cystic fibrosis, and HIV/AIDS may require special education and other related services.	aura hypoglycemia
	Variables affecting the impact of physical disabilities on children's educational performance are severity, age of onset, and visibility.	hyperglycemia cystic fibrosis

Chapter Twelve at a Glance

Main Topics	Key Points	Key Terms
Traumatic Brain Injury (TBI)	TBI is an acquired injury to the brain caused by an external physical force resulting in total or partial functional disability that adversely affects a child's educational performance.	open head injury closed head injury concussion contusions hematoma coma
	Open head injuries are the result of penetration of the skull; closed head injuries are the result of the head hitting an object with such force that the brain slams against the inside of the cranium.	
	Impairments caused by brain injury may be temporary or lasting and fall into three main categories: physical and sensory changes, cognitive impairments, and social, behavior, and emotional problems.	
Educational Approaches	Children with physical disabilities, health impairments, or traumatic brain injury require services from an interdisciplinary team of professionals.	transdisciplinary teams physical therapists occupational therapists orthotists prosthestists assistive technology
	Professionals who may be involved in providing services include: physical therapists, occupational therapists, speech-language pathologists, adaptive physical educators, school nurses, prosthetists, orthotists, health aides, counselors, and medical social workers.	
	Modifications to the physical environment and to classroom activities can enable students with physical and health impairments to participate more fully in the school program.	
	Assistive technology is any piece of equipment or device used to increase, maintain, or improve the functional capabilities of individuals with disabilities.	
	Students with physical limitations should be encouraged to develop as much independence as possible.	
Educational Placement Alternatives	About 40% of students with physical disabilities are served in regular classrooms.	medically fragile
	The amount of supportive help varies greatly according to each child's conditions, needs, and levels of functioning.	
	Successful reentry of children who have missed extended periods of school requires preparation of the child, his parents, and school personnel.	
Current Issues and Future Trends	New and emerging technologies such as bionic body parts and robot assistants offer exciting possibilities for the future.	myoelectric limbs robotics
	Children with physical disabilities can gain self-knowledge and self-confidence by meeting capable adults with disabilities and joining self-advocacy groups.	

Guided Review

I. Physical Disabilities and Health Impairments
   A. Definitions
   - Children with physical disabilities and health conditions who require special education are

     served under two disability categories: _____

   - An orthopedic impairment involves the _____

   - A neuromotor impairment involves the _____

   - According to IDEA, a child is entitled to special education services if _____

     _____

   B. Prevalence
   - Children receiving special education services under the disability category of orthopedic
     impairments and other health impairments represent a little less than _____ of all school-age
     children.
   - Because physical disabilities often occur in combination with _____,
     students with physical disabilities may be served under other categories.
   - There are numerous children whose physical disabilities do not adversely affect

     _____

   C. Types and Causes
   1. Cerebral Palsy
      - CP is the most prevalent physical disability in school-age children.
      - CP is a permanent condition resulting from _____
      - The causes of CP have most often been attributed to injuries, accidents, or illnesses that

        are _____

      - The term "plegia" is often used in combination with a prefix indicating the location of limb
        involvement (e.g., paraplegia, quadriplegia).

      - Spastic cerebral palsy is characterized by _____

      - Athetoid cerebral palsy is characterized by _____

      - Ataxic cerebral palsy is characterized by _____

      - Hypotonia: _____

   2. Spina Bifida

      - Spina bifida is a condition in which the vertebrae do not enclose the _____

      - Spina bifida occulta: _____

      - Meningocele: _____

- Myelomeningocele: _____

- Hydrocephalus: _____

3. Muscular dystrophy
   - Muscular Dystrophy refers to a group of inherited diseases marked by _____

     _____

   - In most cases this disease is fatal in adolescence or young adulthood.

   - Treatment focuses on maintaining function of _____

4. Spinal Cord Injuries
   - Vehicular accidents, sports injuries, and violence are the most common causes in school-age children.
   - The higher the injury on the spine and the more the injury cuts through the spinal cord,

     the greater the _____
   - Rehabilitation programs for children with spinal cord injuries usually involve

     _____

5. Epilepsy: when seizures occur chronically and repeatedly

   - Generalized tonic-clonic seizure: _____

   - Absence seizure: _____

   - Complex partial: _____

   - Simple partial: _____

6. Diabetes: a chronic disorder of metabolism
   - Without proper medical management, the child's system is not able to _____

     _____

   - Hypoglycemia (low blood sugar) symptoms include _____

     _____. Giving the child concentrated
     sugar usually ends the insulin reaction within a few minutes.

   - Hyperglycemia (high blood sugar) symptoms include _____

     _____ . A doctor or nurse should be called immediately.

7. Asthma: a chronic lung disease characterized by wheezing, coughing, and difficulty breathing.
   - most common lung disease of children

   - leading cause of _____ in school

8. Cystic Fibrosis:
   - a genetic disorder in which the exocrine glands excrete thick mucus that can block the

   _____

   - Malnutrition and poor growth are common characteristics of children with cystic fibrosis.

9. Human Immunodeficiency Virus and Acquired Immunodeficiency Syndrome
   - Persons with AIDS are not able to fight off infections because of a breakdown of the immune system.
   - HIV is transmitted through _____

   - Children with HIV/AIDS cannot legally be _____

   _____

   - Because children with HIV/AIDS and their families often face discrimination, teachers and school personnel should actively facilitate school/peer acceptance and school adjustment.

D. Characteristics
   - The characteristics of children with physical disabilities and health impairments are so varied that attempting to describe them is nearly impossible.
   1. Variables Affecting the Impact of Physical Disabilities and Health Impairments on Children's Educational Performance
      - Severity: a severe chronic impairment can greatly limit a child's range of experiences

      - Age of Onset: _____

      _____

      - Visibility: _____

      _____

II. Traumatic Brain Injury
   A. Definition
      - an acquired injury to the brain caused by an external physical force resulting in total or partial functional disability that adversely affects a child's educational performance.

   B. Prevalence
      - TBI is the most common _____ disability in childhood.
      - It is estimated that 1 in 500 school children will be hospitalized with traumatic head injuries, and 1 in 30 children will sustain a significant head injury by age 15.

   C. Types and Causes
      - Open head injury: _____

      - Closed head injury: _____

      - Concussion: _____

      - Hematoma: _____
      - Severe head trauma almost always results in a coma.

D.Characteristics
- Impairments caused by brain injury may be temporary or lasting and fall into three main

  categories: _____

  _____

III. Educational Approaches
  A. Teaming and Related Services
  - transdisciplinary team approach

  - physical therapists: _____

  - occupational therapists: _____
  - Other specialists: speech-language pathologists, adaptive physical educators, school nurses, prosthetists, orthotists, health aides, counselors, and medical social workers

  B. Environmental Modifications
  - Modifications to the physical environment and to classroom activities can enable students with physical and health impairments to participate more fully in the school program.

  C. Assistive Technology
  D. Special Health Care Routines
  E. Independence and Self-esteem

IV. Educational Placement Alternatives
  A. Inclusive Attitudes
  - About 40% of students with physical disabilities are served in _____

  - The amount of supportive help varies greatly according to each child's _____

  _____

  - Some technology-dependent children require home- or hospital-based instruction because their life support equipment cannot be made portable.
  - Successful reentry of children who have missed extended periods of school requires

  preparation of _____

V. Current Issues and Future Trends
  A. Related Services in the Classroom
  B. New and Emerging Technologies for Persons with Severe Physical Disabilities
  C. Animal Assistance
  D. Employment, Life Skills, and Self-Advocacy

In Class Activities

Response Card Activity: Answer the following questions related to physical and health impairments

1. This type of impairment involves bones, joints, limbs, and associated muscles.

2. This is an orthopedic impairment characterized as a disorder of voluntary movement and posture. Some types are hypertonia (spasticity) or hypotonia (floppy muscles).

3. This is an orthopedic impairment in which a portion of the spinal cord and nerves does not develop properly.

4. Children with heart conditions, epilepsy, and ADHD are sometimes served under this category.

5. In order for a child to be served under either the orthopedic or other health impairments category, the disability must also (the second clause in each definition).

6. This is a long-term state in which a child experiences debilitating symptoms.

7. This is a group of inherited diseases marked by progressive atrophy of the muscles.

8. This is a chronic lung disease characterized by bouts of coughing.

9. A child who has cerebral palsy on the right side of her body would be classified as:

10. True or False? Knowing the underlying cause of the student's disability is often helpful in planning special needs services.

11. What are the three most critical variables affecting the impact of a physical disability or other health impairment on a child's development?

12. True or False? The school district must pay for any specialized medical services, provided that a licensed physician does not perform the service.

13. This is an acquired injury to the brain caused by external force.

14. This is an item or piece of equipment used to improve the functional capabilities of a child with a disability.

15. An educational approach in which the teacher works closely with other specialist to provide the most appropriate education possible.

Homework

Write a 2 page position paper on either of the following topics:

1. Inclusion continues to be a major problem for students with physical disabilities. Children with physical and other health impairments are often placed in self-contained special education classes with children who have mental retardation. Do you think this is the best practice? What other options can school systems offer? How do you think general educators and parents feel about placing these children into the general education classroom? If you had a child with severe health impairment, what do you think would be the best placement?

    Resources and Suggestions for Exploration
    U.S. Department of Justice, Disability Rights home page: http://www.usdoj.gov/crt/drs/drshome.htm
    Council for Disability rights: http://www.disabilityrights.org
    Disability rights education and defense fund Inc.: http://www.dredf.org

2. Coping emotionally with a physical disability or health impairment presents a major problem for some children. Maintaining a sense of belonging can be difficult for a child who must frequently leave the classroom to participate in therapeutic or other health care routines. Differences in physical appearance and the need for assistive technology may further cause problems. What role and responsibility does the teacher play in creating an inclusive environment in the classroom? What do you think a teacher should do to help peers and others become more accepting of a student with a physical disability or health impairment?

What Do You Think?
School supports for children with HIV/AIDS

The American Academy of Pediatrics (1994) recommends that most school-age children with HIV/AIDS be allowed to attend public schools without restrictions. Students with HIV/AIDS should attend the regular classroom and be provided with in-class supports (Prater & Serna, 1995). Write a 3-4 page position paper addressing the following questions: What kinds of school supports are most crucial for children with HIV/AIDS? If parents choose to inform the teacher that their child has HIV/AIDS, what are the roles and responsibilities of the teacher? Under what circumstances (if any) should children with HIV/AIDS be placed in environments that are more restrictive than the regular classroom?

Related Sources

Adams, D. R., & Biddle, J. K. (1997). AIDS in the classroom: Are we ready? Journal for a Just and Caring Education, 3, 277-288.

Ford, H. H., & Russo, C. J. (1997). The role of educators in the AIDS epidemic. Journal for a Just & Caring Education, 3, 253-277.

Gilbert, D. J. (2001). HIV-affected children and adolescents: What school social workers should know. Children & Schools, 23, 135-142.

Prater, M. A., & Serna, L. A. (1995). HIV disease. Remedial & Special Education, 16, 68-79.

Sheckler, P. (1992). When a student is HIV positive. Educational Leadership, 50, 55-57.

Sklaire M. (1996). Helping kids live with AIDS. NEA Today, 15, 21-25.

Objectives

PHYSICAL DISABILITIES AND HEALTH IMPAIRMENTS
1. List the key components of the federal definition of orthopedic impairments and other health impairments.
2. Discuss why there are more children with physical impairments and health care needs than those receiving services under those categories.
3. Compare and contrast a chronic condition and an acute condition that adversely affect educational performance.
4. Define and describe the types of disabilities discussed in this chapter.

TRAUMATIC BRAIN INJURY
1. List the key components of the federal definition of traumatic brain injury.
2. List the types and causes of brain injuries.
3. Describe the characteristics and educational needs of children with brain injury.

EDUCATIONAL APPROACHES
1. Describe the various professionals who work with students with physical disabilities and health impairments and their roles and responsibilities.
2. Discuss why collaboration and teaming are especially important with this population of exceptional children.
3. Identify environmental modifications and assistive technology necessary to enable fuller participation in school.

EDUCATIONAL PLACEMENT ALTERNATIVES
1. Identify and provide examples of the continuum of educational placement alternatives for children with physical impairments and special health care needs.

CURRENT ISSUES AND FUTURE TRENDS
1. Identify the key topics related to increased inclusion in society.
2. Describe the new and emerging technology for persons with severe physical disabilities.

Self-check Quiz

True/False

1. Occupational therapists are involved in the development and maintenance of motor skills, movement, and posture.

2. Children with physical disabilities, health impairments, and traumatic brain injury are generally extremely restricted in their activities.

3. When Cheryl tries to sharpen her pencil, her arms wave wildly, she grimaces, and her tongue sticks out, probably indicating athetoid cerebral palsy.

4. A child with chronic asthma does well in school, but needs immediate assistance in the event he has a severe attack. By definition, he is eligible for services as health impaired.

5. Asthma is the leading cause of absenteeism in school.

6. A child with a neuromotor impairment receives service under IDEA as a child with an orthopedic impairment.

7.   Children with contagious diseases, including HIV/AIDS and tuberculosis, were excluded from IDEA protection under the recent reauthorization.

8.   Most traumatic brain injuries do not involve penetration of the skull.

9.   The issue of inclusion of students with physical and health impairments is more one of technology than one of attitude.

10. Parents are required to inform the school if their child has HIV, and certain other serious or contagious health conditions.

11. Related services are of particular importance to children with physical disabilities, health impairments, and traumatic brain injury.

12. Emily had a blow to the head and immediately suffered a seizure. By definition, she has epilepsy.

13. The term "medically fragile" refers to a student dependent upon life-support technology.

14. Recovery from a traumatic brain injury is consistent, i.e., slow at first and usually reaching a plateau which signals the end to expected functional improvement.

15. School districts are not responsible for paying for services such as nursing care or catheterization as they are medical, not educational.

Essay Questions

1.   Describe the characteristics, causes, effects, and treatments of either (a) epilepsy or (b) muscular dystrophy.

2.   Describe Perrin et al.'s (1993) noncategorical system for classifying and understanding children's physical and medical conditions.

CHAPTER THIRTEEN
AUTISM AND SEVERE DISABILITIES

Focus Questions_____

- **Why is a curriculum based on typical developmental stages inappropriate for students with severe disabilities?**

  Developmental theories of learning assume that children pass through an orderly sequence of developmental stages. These stages are the basis for determining what kinds of skills are appropriate for instruction and when those skills should be taught. For example, if a child has not yet developed the physical dexterity necessary to properly hold a pencil, teaching the child to write will usually not begin until the child is developmentally "ready." A curriculum based on typical developmental stages, however, is unlikely to meet the needs of students with severe disabilities. For children with severe disabilities, learning such basic skills as getting from place to place independently, communicating, controlling bowel and bladder functions, and self-feeding cannot wait for a readiness stage to be reached. Instruction in these skills, all of which influence the individual's quality of life, must begin when individuals with severe disabilities need to learn them, not when they are developmentally ready to learn them. The "everyday skills" that normally developing children learn almost effortlessly present substantial challenges for individuals with severe disabilities.

- **Why is it so critical to select functional and age-appropriate curriculum objectives for students with autism or severe disabilities?**

  Students with severe disabilities learn at a much slower rate than typically developing children and have difficulty maintaining and generalizing newly learned behaviors. For this reason, teachers of students with severe disabilities must carefully select and prioritize functional and age-appropriate skills designed to maximize independent functioning. Educational programs for students with severe disabilities are future oriented in their efforts to teach skills that will enable students with severe disabilities to participate in integrated settings as meaningfully and independently as possible after they leave school. Functional and age-appropriate behaviors are more likely to be reinforced in the natural environments, and, as a result, maintained in the student's repertoire.

- **Can a teacher increase the learning potential of students with autism and severe disabilities? How?**

  Children with autism and severe disabilities seldom acquire complex skills through observation and imitation alone. The learning and behavioral problems of students are so extreme and significant that instruction must be carefully planned, systematically executed, and continuously monitored for effectiveness.

- **What are the most important skills for a teacher of students with severe disabilities? Why?**

  Teaching students with severe disabilities is difficult and demanding. The teacher must be well organized, firm, and consistent. He or she must be able to manage a complex educational operation which usually involves supervising paraprofessional aides, student teachers, peer tutors, and volunteers. The teacher must be knowledgeable about instructional formats and be able to work cooperatively with other professionals. Teachers must also be sensitive to and feel rewarded by small positive changes in behavior.

- **How much time should a student with autism or severe disabilities spend in the general education classroom with his or her nondisabled peers?**

  Although the social benefits of regular class participation for students with disabilities have been clearly shown, the effects of full inclusion on the attainment of IEP goals and objectives is not yet known. Available instructional time is especially valuable to students who by definition require direct, intensive, and ongoing instruction to acquire basic skills. A major challenge is to develop models and strategies for including students with severe disabilities without sacrificing opportunities to acquire, practice, and generalize the functional skills they need most.

Essential Concepts

- Often students with severe disabilities need instruction in many basic skills that most children acquire without instruction. However, it is well documented that these students can learn, do learn, and, with appropriate teaching and support, lead productive lives.

- Today a philosophy of inclusion promotes the integration of individuals with severe disabilities into the mainstream of society. This trend is significantly different from the philosophy that promoted institutionalization from infancy.

- No universally accepted definition of severe disabilities exists, and this lack of a precise definition makes prevalence estimates difficult. Although no single set of behaviors is common to all individuals with severe disabilities, this population is often characterized by severe deficits in communication skills, physical and motor development, self-help skills, and excesses of maladaptive or inappropriate behavior.

- The causes of severe disabilities are often traced to biological influences that result in brain damage. Chromosomal abnormalities, genetic disorders, complications during pregnancy or the birthing process, as well as head trauma and disease later in life, can all cause severe disabilities. The specific cause of many severely disabling conditions, however, is not known.

- Educational programming for students with severe disabilities has changed dramatically from the not-so-distant past when automatic institutionalization and little or no instruction or training were the norm. Today, least restrictive educational placements are mandated, and the trend is toward educating students with severe disabilities in regular school settings.

- Individuals with severe disabilities present many challenges to the field of special education, but these challenges should not be viewed as burdens. Most of us do our best work when faced with challenges that demand our best. Educating students with severe disabilities is a dynamic, changing area of special education that influences the direction of the field as a whole. The opportunity to work with individuals with severe disabilities can provide tremendous personal and professional rewards.

Chapter Thirteen at a Glance

Main Topics	Key Points	Key Terms
Autism	Autism is a disability marked by severe impairment of communication and social and emotional functioning.	Asperger's syndrome affect isolation self-stimulation savant syndrome
	Characteristics of children with autism include: apparent sensory deficit, severe affect isolation, self-stimulation, tantrums and self-mutilatory behavior, echolalic and psychotic speech, and behavior deficiencies.	
	The Autism Society of America estimates that autism occurs in as many as 1 in 500 children.	
	Although the precise cause of autism is unknown, recent research shows a clear biological and organic origin.	
	Intensive, behaviorally based early intervention has helped some children with autism learn communication and social skills.	
Severe Disabilities	Severe disabilities are defined by significant disabilities in intellectual, physical, and/or social functioning.	profound disabilities multiple disabilities deaf-blindness stereotypic behavior brain dysgenesis
	Students with severe disabilities need instruction in basic skills, communicating with others, controlling bowel and bladder functions, and self-feeding.	
	Multiple disabilities means concomitant impairments, the combination of which causes such severe educational problems that they cannot be accommodated in special education program solely for one impairment.	
	The majority of children who have both visual and hearing impairments at birth experience major difficulties in acquiring communication and motor skills, mobility, and appropriate social behavior.	
	Characteristics of severe disabilities include: slow acquisition rates for learning new skills, poor generalization and maintenance of newly learned skills, limited communication skills, impaired physical and motor development, deficits in self-help skills, infrequent constructive behavior and interaction, and stereotypic and challenging behavior.	
	Because there is no universally accepted definition of severe disabilities, there are no accurate and uniform figures on prevalence. Estimates range from 0.1% to 1% of the population.	
	In almost every case of severe disabilities, a brain disorder is involved.	

Chapter Thirteen at a Glance

Main Topics	Key Points	Key Terms
Educational Approaches	Curriculum goals for students with severe disabilities should be functional and age-appropriate. Students with severe disabilities should be taught choice-making skills, communication skills, and recreation and leisure skills.	functionality partial participation positive behavioral support functional assessment
	Because each student with autism and severe disabilities has many learning needs, teachers must carefully prioritize and choose IEP objectives and learning activities that will be of most benefit to the student and his family.	
	Partial Participation is both a philosophy for selecting activities and a method for adapting activities and supports to enable students with severe disabilities to actively participate in meaningful tasks they are not able to perform independently.	
	The teacher of students with severe disabilities must be skilled in positive, instructionally relevant strategies for assessing and dealing with challenging and problem behaviors.	
	Elements of positive behavioral support include understanding the meaning that a behavior has for a student, teaching the student a positive alternative behavior, using environmental restructuring to make undesired behaviors less likely, and using strategies that are socially acceptable and intended for use in integrated settings.	
	Research and practice are providing increasing support for the use of integrated small-group instruction arrangements with students with severe disabilities.	
	Students with severe disabilities are more likely to develop social relationships with students without disabilities if they are included at least part of the time in the regular classroom.	
	Although the initial reactions of many general education teachers are negative, those apprehensions often transform into positive experiences.	
The Challenge and Rewards of Teaching Students with Autism and Severe Disabilities	Teachers of students with severe disabilities must be sensitive to small changes in behavior.	
	The effective teacher is consistent and persistent in evaluating and changing instruction to improve learning and behavior.	
	Working with students who require instruction at its very best can be highly rewarding to teachers.	

Guided Review

I. Autism
   A. Definition
      • Autism is a disability marked by severe impairment of _____

      _____

   B. Characteristics

      • apparent _____

      • severe _____
      • self-stimulation

      • tantrums and _____

      • echolalic and _____
      • behavior deficiencies

   C. Prevalence
      • The Autism Society of America estimates that autism occurs in as many as _____

   D. Causes of Autism
      • Although the precise cause of autism is unknown, recent research shows a _____

      _____

   E. Effective Treatment for Children with Autism
      • Intensive, behaviorally based early intervention has helped some children with autism learn

      _____

II. Severe Disabilities
   A. Definitions
      • Significant disabilities in _____

      • Students with severe disabilities need instruction in_ _____

      _____

      • An individual with profound disabilities functions at a level no higher than that of a typically developing 2-year-old .

   B. Multiple Disabilities and Deaf-Blindness

      • Multiple disabilities means _____ impairments, the combination of which causes such severe educational problems that they cannot be accommodated in a special education program solely for one impairment.

- The majority of children who have both visual and hearing impairments at birth experience

   major difficulties in_____

   _____

C. Characteristics
- slow acquisition rates for _____

- poor generalization and _____

- limited _____

- impaired _____

- deficits in _____

- infrequent constructive _____

- stereotypic and _____

D. Prevalence
- Because there is no universally accepted definition of severe disabilities, there are no accurate and uniform figures on prevalence.

- Estimates range from _____ of the population

E. Causes
- In almost every case of severe disabilities, a _____ is involved.
- A significant percentage of children with severe disabilities are born with chromosomal disorders or with genetic or metabolic disorders that can cause serious problems in physical or intellectual development.
- Severe disabilities may develop later in life from _____

- In about one-sixth of all cases, the cause _____

III. Educational Approaches
   A. Curriculum: What Should Be Taught?
      1. Functionality
      2. Age-appropriateness
      3. Making Choices
      4. Communication Skills
      5. Recreation and Leisure Skills

   B. Instructional Methods: How Should Students Be Taught?

- The student's current level of performance must be _____

- The skill to be taught must be _____

- The skill may need to be broken down into _____

- The teacher must provide a clear _____

- The student must receive _____

- Strategies that promote _____

- The student's performance must be _____

1. Partial Participation
   - Even though some individuals are not able to independently perform all steps of a given

     task, they can be taught to _____

2. Positive Behavioral Support: Elements of Positive Behavioral Support include

   - understanding the _____

   - teaching the student a _____

   - using environmental restructuring to make _____

   - using strategies that are socially acceptable and _____

3. Small Group Instruction

   - Skills learned in small groups may be more likely to _____

   - provides opportunities for _____

   - provides opportunities for incidental or observation learning from _____

   - may be a more cost-effective use of _____

C. Where Should Students with Severe Disabilities Be Taught?
   1. Benefits of the Neighborhood School
      - more likely to function responsibly as _____

      - integrated schools are more _____

      - parents and families have _____

      - develop range of relationships with _____

   2. Social Relationships
      - Students with severe disabilities are more likely to develop social relationships with students without disabilities if they are included at least part of the time in the regular classroom

   3. Experiences and Transformations of General Education Teachers
      - Although the initial reactions of many general education teachers are negative, those apprehensions often transform into positive experiences.

   4. How Much Time in the Regular Classroom?

IV. The Challenge and Rewards of Teaching Students with Autism and Severe Disabilities

- Teachers must be sensitive to _____

- The effective teacher is consistent and persistent in _____

   _____

- Working with students who require instruction at its very best can be _____

In Class Activity

Small Group Activity: Identify functional skills

After reading the PROFILES & PERSPECTIVES segment, "My Brother Darryl: A Case for Teaching Functional Skills," work together with your group to generate a list of appropriate objectives for the 18-year-old with severe disabilities. Be sure your objectives are age-appropriate and functional. After generating your list, sequentially prioritize your objectives in terms of what you think should be taught first. Present your list of objectives to the whole class, and provide a rationale for the selection and sequence of objectives your group generated.

Homework

Re-read the PROFILES & PERSPECTIVES feature, "Are All Children Educable?" Think about how your views about least restrictive environment, inclusion, and normalization have developed throughout the preceding chapters. How do your views about these issues change as the severity of an individual's disability increases? Write a two page paper examining your position.

What Do You Think?
Should skin shock be used to decrease or eliminate self-injurious behavior?

Many children with severe disabilities and autism engage in self-injurious behavior. The use of skin shock has been demonstrated to be effective for decreasing self-injury. However, the Association for Persons with Severe Handicaps (TASH) has been calling for the elimination of the use of all aversive procedures (including skin shock) to control individuals with disabilities. Write a 3-4 page position paper explaining the extent to which and under what circumstances (if any) self-injurious behavior should be controlled by skin shock or any other aversive procedure.

Related Issues to consider:
TASH points out some of the following reasons to avoid aversive control for self-injury:
- dehumanization of the individual
- potential or actual side effects such as tissue damage, physical illness, or emotional stress
- discomfort on the part of family members, staff, or caregivers
- rebellion on the part of the person engaging in self-injury

Do you think using skin shock is more humane than allowing a child to be put in restraints or to continue severely hurting himself?

Resources and Suggestions for Exploration

TASH: Toward the Elimination of the Use of Aversive Procedures to Control Individuals with Disabilities
http://www.oaksgroup.org/action/index.htm

Self-Injurious Behavior: Examination of Causation and Treatment
http://www.aet.cup.edu/~edp656/stefl/sib.htm#behavorial

A Remote-Controlled Electric Shock Device for Behavior Modification
http://www.effectivetreatment.org/remote.html

Comparison of the Long-term Decelerative Effectiveness of Two Intensities of Contingent Electric Shock on Aggressive and Health Dangerous Behavior with Individuals with Severe Behavioral Disorders
http://www.effectivetreatment.org/comp.html

Comments by parents on use of skin shock: http://www.effectivetreatment.org/comments.html

Objectives

AUTISM
1. Define autism.
2. List the 6 behavioral characteristics often associated with autism.
3. Identify and describe effective treatments for students with autism.

SEVERE DISABILITIES
1. Define severe disabilities.
2. Define multiple disabilities.
3. List the common characteristics of students with severe disabilities.

PREVALENCE
1. Discuss the 2 reasons why determining prevalence data is difficult.

CAUSES
1. List the probable causes for some types of severe disabilities.

EDUCATIONAL APPROACHES
1. List the 3 questions that must be answered when considering curriculum.
2. List the major curriculum areas.
3. Identify and provide examples of effective instructional methods.
4. List the components of functional assessment.
5. Discuss the benefits to teaching students with severe disabilities in the local school.

THE CHALLENGES AND REWARDS OF TEACHING STUDENTS WITH SEVERE DISABILITIES
1. Discuss the challenges and rewards of teaching students with severe disabilities.

Self-check Quiz

True/False

1. Therapies for autism which have scientifically validated support include applied behaviorism, facilitated communication, and megavitamin therapy.

2. Having autism often precludes meaningful achievements.

3. Children with profound disabilities are usually classified via intelligence tests.

4. Most individuals with autism also have intellectual impairments.

5. Lovaas's (1987) study seems to indicate that few children with autism can make significant gains in communication or social skills.

6. Recreation and leisure skills are a necessary part of curriculum for children with severe disabilities.

7. IDEA specifies very limited circumstances under which a child is not considered educable (e.g., is comatose) and therefore not entitled to an education.

8. Most individuals with autism appear to have normal development during their first year of life.

9. Geoff has blindness as well as cerebral palsy. He is best described as having severe disabilities.

10. There are crucial distinctions between children with profound disabilities and those with severe disabilities.

11. With early, appropriate intervention, the prognosis for autism is good.

12. Teachers of students with autism and severe disabilities must prioritize instructional targets for skill deficits rather than target all at once.

13. Girls are as likely as boys to be affected by autism.

14. "Naturalistic teaching" refers to teachers systematically providing feedback to students when they spontaneously demonstrate a skill.

15. Most severe disabilities are caused by trauma at birth or in later accidents.

Essay Questions

1. Describe the general characteristics of autism, including those characteristics associated with the disorder but not necessarily present.

2. Describe the characteristics of individuals who are deaf-blind, and offer a rationale as to why this remains a separate disability category.

CHAPTER FOURTEEN
GIFTEDNESS AND TALENT

Focus Questions

- **Why do students who are very bright need special education?**

Special education is necessary for children when their physical attributes and/or learning abilities differ from the norm to such an extent that an individualized program of special education is required to meet their needs. When a traditional classroom curriculum is not allowing children who are gifted and talented to fulfill their potential and to succeed fully in school, then special education is needed.

- **How has the evolving definition of giftedness changed the ways in which students are identified and served?**

Intelligence, creativity, and talent have been central to the various definitions that have been proposed over the years, and they continue to be reflected in the current and still-evolving definitions. Historically, however, the concept of giftedness has been neither as broad nor as inclusive as the definitions we currently use. According to most early definitions, only those individuals with outstanding performances on standard intelligence tests were considered gifted. This narrow view of giftedness dominated by an IQ score prevailed for many years and came to be associated with only the Caucasian, urban, and middle- and upper-class segments of society. Current definitions have grown out of our awareness that IQ alone does not define all the possible areas of giftedness. Today's definitions include many talents that contribute substantially to the quality of life for both the individual and society. This more comprehensive definition allows us to identify and serve a more diverse group of gifted learners.

- **What provisions should be made to accurately identify students with outstanding talents who are from diverse cultural groups or have disabilities?**

Biases inherent in the identification process are primarily to blame for the underrepresentation of students from culturally diverse groups in programs for the gifted. Today more so than ever, we recognize the need for culturally non-biased identification and assessment practices. Current "best practices" for identifying these students from diverse cultural groups involves obtaining information from a variety of sources such as portfolios of student work, tests in specific content areas, creativity tests, and problem-solving tests. Maker (1994) developed a procedure called DISCOVER that is used to assess gifted students from diverse backgrounds, female students, and students with disabilities. The DISCOVER assessment process involves a series of five progressively more complex problems that provide children with various ways to demonstrate problem-solving competence.

- **In what ways should the pace and depth of curriculum be differentiated for gifted and talented students?**

Three common approaches to educating students who are gifted and talented are curriculum compacting, enrichment, and acceleration. Some experts advocate the development of an individualized growth plan to develop a broad program of services for gifted and talented students. The growth plan should include assessment information, student-generated goals, and the recommended activities for accomplishing these goals. A key ingredient of this approach is that the student is an active participant in all instructional and evaluative activities. Similar to the IEP, a growth plan could be used to guide the teacher in the development of appropriate lessons for the gifted and talented while at the same time meeting the needs of the other students. In addition, recent advancement in technology could be used to help further individualize the gifted student's program.

- **How can grouping help the regular classroom teacher plan for the educational needs of students of various abilities while at the same time meeting the needs of other students in the classroom?**

  Although ability grouping has been an issue of considerable debate, it is one strategy that might enable regular classroom teachers to appropriately differentiate instruction in order to meet the needs of the wide range of abilities represented in a classroom. Grouping enables gifted students to be appropriately challenged through more rapid and advanced instruction. Allowing gifted students to be grouped so that they can progress at their own pace may preserve the students' motivation to learn and help prevent problems such as boredom and an aversion towards school.

Essential Concepts

- Gifted and talented children represent the other end on the continuum of academic, artistic, social, and scientific abilities. Just as the traditional curriculum is often inappropriate for the child with a disability, it also can be inappropriate for the child who is gifted and talented. The traditional curriculum may not provide the kinds of challenges the student who is gifted requires to learn most effectively. As a result, these students may represent the most underserved group of exceptional children.

- Numerous definitions of gifted and talented have been proposed and debated over the years. The first definitions focused solely on intellectual abilities as measured by IQ tests. More recent definitions have sought to encompass broader perspectives. The current definition has eliminated "giftedness" as a descriptive characteristic and further de-emphasized IQ.

- Evidence of how the definition has changed is found in the way talented children are identified and assessed. Current assessment approaches are multifactored and include data from a variety of sources including work portfolios and teacher and peer nominations, as well as traditional IQ and achievement tests. However, biases may still exist in the assessment process as evidenced by the underrepresentation of some minority groups.

- Three common educational approaches for talented students are curriculum: enrichment, compacting, and acceleration. Enrichment experiences are those that let students investigate topics of interest in much greater detail. Curriculum compacting is compressing the instructional content so that academically able students have more time to work on more challenging materials. Acceleration is the general term for modifying the pace at which the student moves through the curriculum.

- If the long-range needs of the society are to be met, it must capitalize on one of its most precious human resources-children who are gifted and talented. Given the opportunities to reach their potential, many of these children will contribute to the quality of our collective future. Of more immediate concern, and perhaps even more importantly, the educational needs of these exceptional children must be met because they are deserving of an appropriate education.

Chapter Fourteen at a Glance

Main Topics	Key Points	Key Terms
Defining Giftedness and Talent	The federal definition of gifted and talented includes the following features: high performance capability in intellectual, creative, and/or artistic areas, an unusual leadership capacity; or excelling in specific academic fields. Other contemporary definitions of giftedness include Renzulli's three-trait definition, Piirto's Pyramid, and Sternberg's Triarchic Model.	general intellectual ability specific academic talent
Characteristics of Gifted and Talented Students	Children who are gifted rapidly acquire, retain, and use large amounts of information; relate ideas; make sound judgments; perceive the operation of larger systems; acquire and manipulate abstract symbol systems; and solve problems by creating novel solutions. The unusual talents and abilities of gifted students may make them either withdrawn or difficult to manage in the classroom. Gifted and highly talented individuals are found across gender, cultural, linguistic, and disability groups. Characteristics of highly gifted students (IQ>145) may include intense intellectual curiosity, perfectionism, need for precision, learning in intuitive leaps, intense need for mental stimulation, difficulty conforming, early moral/existential concern, and a tendency towards introversion. Dimensions of creative behavior include fluency, flexibility, novelty/originality, elaboration, synthesizing ability, analyzing ability, ability to reorganize or redefine existing ideas, and complexity.	interindividual intraindividual divergent production fluency flexibility novelty/originality elaboration synthesizing ability analyzing ability
Prevalence	The most commonly cited prevalence estimate is that high IQ students make up 3% to 5% of the population. There are many forms of talent that do not require a high IQ, and 10%-15% of students may possess such talents.	normal curve social construct
Identification and Assessment	The usual means of identification in a multifactored assessment include IQ tests; achievement tests; portfolios; and teacher, parent, self, and peer nomination. Biases inherent in the identification process are primarily to blame for the underrepresentation of minority students receiving services for gifted education. Maker's DISCOVER procedure can be used to equitably identify students from diverse cultural groups.	Precocity

Chapter Fourteen at a Glance

Main Topics	Key Points	Key Terms
Curriculum and Instruction	Curriculum for gifted students should be based on learning characteristics of academically talented students, possess academic rigor, be thematic and interdisciplinary, consider various curriculum orientations, and be balanced and articulated.	Differentiated curriculum acceleration enrichment curriculum compacting tiered lessons Bloom's Taxonomy interdependence
	Acceleration (moving through the curriculum faster) and enrichment (probing subject matter in greater depth) are ways to modify the curriculum for gifted students.	
	Curriculum compacting involves compressing the instructional content and materials so that academically advanced students have more time to work on challenging materials.	
	Tiered lessons provide different extensions of the same basic lesson for groups of students with differing abilities.	
	Bloom's Taxonomy provides a framework for differentiating instruction and uses six levels of learning: knowledge, comprehension, application, analysis, synthesis, and evaluation.	
	Curriculum differentiation outside the classroom may include internships and mentor programs, special courses, competitions, summer programs, and international experiences.	
	Three models for differentiating curriculum include the Schoolwide Enrichment Model, Maker's Active Problem Solver Model, and the Problem-based Learning units.	
Educational Placement Alternatives and Ability Grouping	Students who are gifted may receive services in special schools, self-contained classrooms, resource rooms, and regular classrooms. There are advantages and disadvantages to each type of educational placement.	Ability grouping tracking within-class grouping cluster groups cross-grade grouping
	A teacher with special training may work with the regular classroom teacher as a consultant who collaborates to help plan multi-level lessons.	
	Many schools do not have a specialist, and the regular classroom teacher is responsible for differentiating the curriculum.	
Current Issues and Future Trends	The definitional nature of giftedness is being more intensely questioned.	
	We need better procedures for identifying, assessing, teaching, and encouraging these children. We must improve society's attitudes toward gifted and talented children if we are to improve their futures.	

Guided Review

I. Defining Giftedness and Talent
   A. Federal Definitions
   - These children exhibit high performance capability in intellectual, creative, and/or artistic

     areas, possess an unusual leadership capacity, or _____

   B. Other Key Contemporary and Complementary Definitions

   - Renzulli's Three Trait Definition: _____

     _____

   - Piirto's Pyramid Model: a foundation of genetic endowment, personality attributes, intelligence, talent in a specific domain, environmental influences.

   - Sternberg's Triarchic Model: _____

II. Characteristics of Gifted and Talented Students
   - Gifted and highly talented individuals are found across _____

     _____

     Characteristics of highly gifted students (IQ>145): _____

     _____

     _____

   A. Individual Differences among Gifted and Talented Students
   - Awareness of individual differences is important in understanding gifted students.

   B. Creativity: dimensions of cognitive creative behavior

   - fluency: _____

   - flexibility: _____

   - novelty/originality: _____

   - elaboration: _____

   - synthesizing ability: _____

   - analyzing ability: _____

   - ability to reorganize or redefine existing ideas

   - complexity: _____

III. Prevalence
   - Gifted and talented children comprise about 5% of the school-age population.
   - Gifted and talented children may be the most underserved group of exceptional children.

IV. Identification and Assessment
- A multifactored assessment approach uses information from a variety of sources including:

_____

A. Multicultural Assessment and Identification
- Biases inherent in the identification process are primarily to blame for the _____

_____

_____
- Maker's DISCOVER procedure can be used to equitably identify students from diverse cultural groups.

B. Gifted and Talented Girls
- Cultural barriers; testing and social biases; organizational reward systems; sex role stereotyping; and conflicts among career and family all act as _____

_____

C. Gifted and Talented Boys
- Being gifted puts a burden on boys, not only to prove their masculinity, but also _____

_____

D. Gifted and Talented Students with Disabilities
- The combination of a disability and giftedness brings with it _____

_____

V. Curriculum and Instruction
A. Curricular Goals: Curriculum for gifted students should
- be based on learning characteristics of academically talented students

- possess _____

- be thematic and _____

- consider various _____
- be balanced and articulated

B. Differentiating the Curriculum: Acceleration and Enrichment
- Acceleration is permitting a student to _____ (e.g., grade skipping, mentorships, advanced placement, credit by examination).

- Enrichment experiences let students _____

C. Other Methods for Differentiating Curriculum and Instruction
- Curriculum compacting involves compressing the instructional content and materials so that

academically able students have _____
- Tiered lessons provide different extensions of the same basic lesson for _____

_____

- Bloom's Taxonomy provides a useful framework for differentiating instruction. The six levels

  of learning are: _____

  _____

D. Curriculum Differentiation Outside the Classroom
    - Internships and mentor programs
    - Special Courses
    - Competitions
    - Junior Great Books
    - Summer Programs
    - International Experiences

E. Three Curriculum Models for Gifted Education
    1. Schoolwide Enrichment Model
        - an umbrella under which many different types of _____
          are made available to gifted students and all other students

        - relevant features: _____

          _____

          _____

    2. Maker's Active Problem Solver Model
        - The role of the teacher is to facilitate high achievement by making four types of

          _____

    3. Problem-based Learning
        - Students work cooperatively in groups to seek solutions _____
        - Instructional units give students experience in collecting, organizing, analyzing, and

          _____

VI. Educational Placement Alternatives and Ability Grouping
    A. Special Schools

    B. Self-contained Classrooms
        - The primary advantage is that _____

          _____

        - Self-contained classroom programs for gifted students often must deal with stigma of _____

          _____

        - Some districts may be too small to support this option.

    C. Resource Room or Pullout Programs
        - still need to differentiate the curriculum when _____

    D. Regular Classroom
        - A teacher with special training may work with the _____

        - Collaborating on curriculum planning teams helps _____

        - Many schools do not have a specialist, and the regular classroom teacher is responsible for

          _____

E.   Ability Grouping
   • Most educators and researchers in the field of gifted education advocate for ability grouping.

   • XYZ Grouping or Tracking places students into different levels of _____

   • Potential dangers of tracking (low expectations, limited learning opportunities in lower tracks)

     have caused some critics to call for_____
   • Students can also be grouped for instruction within a class.
   • Cross-grade grouping for selected subjects (e.g., reading)
   • Guidelines for ability grouping:
     1.   resist calls for the wholesale elimination of _____

     2.   maintain programs of _____

     3.   maintain programs of _____
     4.   Schools should try to adjust the curriculum to the aptitude level of the groups.
     5.   Benefits are slight from programs that group children by ability but prescribe common
          curricular experiences for all ability groups.

VII. Current Issues and Future Trends
   • The conceptual and definitional nature of giftedness is being _____

   • Most services for gifted and talented students will probably originate from _____

     _____
   • We need better procedures for identifying, assessing, teaching, and encouraging these children.
   • We must improve society's attitudes toward gifted and talented children if we are to improve their
     futures.

In Class Activities

Small Group Activity: Identify enrichment and acceleration activities

Generate with the members of your group a list of activities that would be appropriate for gifted students. Identify your activities as either enrichment or acceleration activities.

Small Group Activity: Define giftedness

Work with a group of four students to develop your own definition of giftedness. After you have developed your definition, develop a multifactored assessment instrument for identifying students who are gifted and talented. Describe how your instrument is related to your group's definition.

Response Card Activity: Identify the level of Bloom's Taxonomy

Identify each objective as one of the following levels of Bloom's Taxonomy: knowledge, comprehension, application, analysis, synthesis, or evaluation.

1. David will state the definitions of the following vocabulary words: precipitation, humidity, Fahrenheit.

2. Helen will explain the meanings of the following vocabulary words in her own words: monopoly, cartel, conglomerate.

3. Joanne will write a sentence with each of the following vocabulary words: responsibility, privilege, justice.

4. Neil will explain how the meanings of the following words are alike and how they are different: dispute, debate, quarrel, altercation.

5. Brian will count to ten in Spanish.

6. Jason will explain the meanings of each of the amendments in the Bill of Rights in his own words.

7. Kathy will describe specific examples of how the first amendment protects citizens in our current culture.

8. Diane will state her opinion about which amendments to the Bill of Rights are the most important and will support her opinion with facts.

9. Darlene will identify the names of coins.

10. Pete will make purchases using the correct combinations of dollars and coins and make sure he gets the correct amount of change from his purchases.

11. Mark will be given a hypothetical income and create a budget for himself.

12. Danielle will read story problems and decide whether she is required to add, subtract, multiply, or divide.

13. Richard will research whales and write a report using correct mechanics and expository writing.

14. Cecilia will use a ruler to measure lines of different lengths.

15. Michael will be presented with various items to measure and will select the most appropriate measurement tool.

Homework

Develop a brief assessment designed to measure creativity. After reviewing the definitions of each dimension of creativity identified by Guilford (1987) in Chapter 14, create one assessment task for each dimension. For example, "fluency" means the person is capable of producing many ideas per unit of time. So an example of an assessment for fluency might be, "Tell me as many uses for a paper clip that you can think of in one minute."

1. fluency
2. flexibility
3. novelty/originality
4. elaboration
5. synthesizing ability
6. analyzing ability
7. ability to reorganize or redefine existing ideas
8. complexity

What Do You Think?
Differentiation in the Regular Classroom and the Achievement of Gifted/Talented Students

As you read this chapter, don't have any doubt-you *will* have gifted and talented students in your classroom. They are the most underserved population of special needs students. In order to meet their academic needs, you will have to differentiate. Choose a grade level, choose a subject, choose a topic, and practice tiering a lesson (see Figure 14.8). Include how you will assess the lesson. Alternately, you may choose to take a common story and practice your questioning techniques according to Bloom's Taxonomy (see Figure 14.9).

Resources and Suggestions for Exploration

Tomlinson, C.A. (1995). The differentiated classroom: Responding to the needs of all learners. Arlington, VA: Association for Supervision and Curriculum Development.

Differentiation Exemplars
http://www.mcps.k12.md.us/departments/eii/diffexemplaryex.html

Differentiated Instruction for the Gifted
http://www.kidsource.com/kidsource/content/diff_instruction.html

Literature in Education-Differentiated Instruction
http://www.teach-nology.com/litined/dif_instruction/

Tips for the Classroom: Extending Learning for Students Who Exceed Standards
http://www.lincolncity.com/agp/teachtips.htm

Differentiated Instruction
http://tst1160-35.k12.fsu.edu/mainpage.html

The Learning Environment
http://www.nwrel.org/msec/just_good/9/ch5.html

Teaching in Mixed Ability Classrooms
http://www.weac.org/kids/1998-99/march99/differ.htm

Objectives

DEFINING GIFTEDNESS AND TALENT
1. List the components of the federal (IDEA) definition of talented children.
2. Compare and contrast the Maker, Renzullli, Piirto, and Sternberg definitions of giftedness.

CHARACTERISTICS OF STUDENTS WHO ARE GIFTED AND TALENTED
1. Define and provide examples of common behavioral characteristics of students who demonstrate outstanding abilities.

PREVALENCE
1. List the prevalence figures for children who demonstrate outstanding abilities.

IDENTIFICATION AND ASSESSMENT
1. Identify the components of a multifactored assessment.

EDUCATIONAL APPROACHES
1. Define and provide examples of curriculum enrichment, compacting, and acceleration.

EDUCATIONAL PLACEMENT ALTERNATIVES
1. Describe the continuum of educational placements for students who are gifted.

CURRENT ISSUES AND FUTURE TRENDS
1. Discuss the reasons why researchers de-emphasize giftedness.

Self-check Quiz

True/False

1. The universally accepted definition of creativity is that offered in Guilford's Structure of Intellect model.

2. Dion has the reading and writing abilities of a student 5 years older than himself but has mathematics abilities at grade level, reflecting intraindividual differences.

3. Precocity refers to achievements resembling those of older children.

4. The primary limitation of early federal attempts to define giftedness is that superior intellectual ability was the sole criterion.

5. Piirto's perspective is that the specific talents of highly gifted children should be nurtured toward fields productive to society such as inventors, physicians, artists, etc.

6. The current federal definition of gifted and talented children is not from IDEA, but rather the "National Excellence" report.

7. Giftedness ranks as the fourth largest group of children receiving special education services.

8. As criteria for identification as gifted and talented have become less exclusive, it's likely that more children are identified than actually need services.

9.   Each state has its own identification procedures and criteria for gifted and talented students.

10. Underrepresentation of children from groups such as African-Americans and Latinos in gifted programs is primarily due to lack of parent and teacher initiation of the identification process.

11. An increasingly popular approach for identifying gifted and talented children is the multidimensional screening approach.

12. The incidence of giftedness and talent among a large proportion of students with disabilities is similar to that of the general population.

13. Curriculum compacting refers to a process of condensing material in scope and sequence.

14. Allowing a student to skip grades, or to gain early entrance into college, are examples of acceleration.

15. The concept of special schools for the gifted and talented has only recently been introduced, given that exceptionality historically emphasized disability.

Essay Questions

1.   Compare and contrast the terms acceleration and enrichment, providing two examples of each in practice.

2.   Compare and contrast the Schoolwide Enrichment, Maker's Active Problem Solver, and Problem-Based Learning models of gifted education.

CHAPTER FIFTEEN
TRANSITION TO ADULTHOOD

*Focus Questions*_____

- **What can teachers of elementary children with disabilities do to help prepare them for successful lives as adults?**

According to IDEA, a statement of transition service needs must be included in a student's IEP beginning at age 14, and an Individual Transition Plan must be developed by age 16. However, preparing students with disabilities to function successfully in the real world should begin as early as possible. Teachers can begin preparing elementary children with disabilities for adulthood by targeting skills such as social interaction, functional academics (e.g., telling time, counting money), daily living (e.g., eating habits, self-care), and choice making. Additionally, teachers should expose students to the variety of career opportunities and leisure activities available to them.

- **Why should post-school outcomes drive education programming for secondary students with disabilities?**

When developing an Individual Transition Plan for secondary students with disabilities, the question guiding the selection of each objective should be, "Will the student need this skill when he's 21?" The goal of transition planning is to enable the student to function as independently as possible when he becomes an adult. The multidisciplinary team should select only the goals and objectives that will contribute to post-school success of the student with disabilities.

- **What are the most important factors in determining the success of an individualized transition plan?**

Teaming and collaboration are absolutely critical when planning and delivering services for secondary students with disabilities. The factors most likely to determine the success of an individualized transition plan include the student's involvement, family involvement, and collaboration by the professionals involved. Cooperation and communication between and among professionals and families are critical to effective transition planning.

- **How can programs such as sheltered employment and group homes, which are intended to help adults with disabilities, limit their participation in and enjoyment of adulthood?**

In the process of creating teaching and working environments that promote success for individuals with disabilities, we sometimes fail to adequately prepare them to live and work in more normalized settings. How? We create teaching and learning environments that are significantly different from more normalized settings, thereby limiting opportunities to participate in more normalized settings. As a result, attempts at integration into normalized settings are unsuccessful. Even though all individuals with disabilities will not likely achieve full independence in their communities, special education must plan its instruction to provide every opportunity for the achievement of independent adult living by individuals with disabilities.

- **Should quality of life for adults with disabilities be the ultimate outcome measure for special education?**

  Ultimately, quality of life **should** be the outcome measure of all educational programs, including those programs for students with disabilities. A person may have been taught many skills, but if those skills do not enable him to enjoy the benefits available in personal, social, work, and leisure settings, the wrong skills have been taught and a disservice has been done to that individual. When selecting and prioritizing specific skills to teach students with disabilities, teachers must consider the extent to which those skills will ultimately help improve the student's quality of life.

Essential Concepts

- Although American society has come a long way with regard to the opportunities afforded young adults with disabilities, it has been estimated that as many as 30% of special education students drop out of school before graduation. In addition, former special education students are more likely to be under- or unemployed after they exit school than are non-special education age mates. Thus, there is a long way to go in developing effective transition-to-adulthood programming and in improving society's attitudes toward the integration of adults with disabilities into work settings.

- Because so many professionals have dedicated themselves to learning more about effective programming for transition into adulthood, there are more exceptional adults than ever working, living, and enjoying leisure activities in community-based, integrated settings. In the not too distant past, the opportunity for adults with disabilities to earn competitive wages for meaningful work was almost nonexistent. Today, a type of vocational opportunity referred to as supported employment enables individuals with severe disabilities to participate successfully in integrated settings.

- In addition to educating individuals with disabilities in work and independent-living skills, many professionals realize the importance of teaching recreation and leisure skills. Learning appropriate recreational and leisure-time activities is difficult for many adults with disabilities.

- Increased community-based residential services for adults with disabilities have meant a greater opportunity to live in more normalized settings. Three residential alternatives for adults with mental retardation and related developmental disabilities-group homes, foster homes, and semi-independent apartment living-help to complete the continuum of possible living arrangements between the segregated, public institution and fully independent living.

- The quality of life for most adults with disabilities in the new millennium is better than it has ever been. Over the past 25 years, adults with mental retardation have been moving from large institutions into smaller, more normalized, community-based living environments. Increasingly, these adults are employed in integrated settings. Special education has come a long way in educating exceptional children to be better prepared for the challenges and joys of being an adult. In addition, society at large is providing more of the same opportunities to these adults. There, however, remains much work to be done.

Chapter Fifteen at a Glance

Main Topics	Key Points	Key Terms
How Do Former Special Education Students Fare as Adults?	The unemployment rate for young adults with disabilities who have been out of school for less than two years is 46%, and 36.5% when they have been out of school for 3 to 5 years.	
	Most young adults who had found competitive employment were working part-time, low-paying jobs.	
	Although the percentage of college students who indicate they have a disability has increased in recent years, compared to their peers without disabilities, fewer former special education students pursue postsecondary education.	
	Four out of five former special education students had still not achieved the status of independent adulthood after being out of high school for up to 5 years.	
Transition Services and Models	Transition from school to life in the community has become perhaps the most challenging issue in special education today.	Individual Transition Plan
	Models for school to adult life transition stress the importance of a functional secondary school curriculum that provides work experience in integrated community job sites, systematic cooperation between school and adult service agencies, parental involvement and support, and a written individual transition plan to guide the entire process.	
	Examples of transition models are Will's Bridges Model of School-to-Work Transition and Halpern's Three-dimensional Model.	
	Transition Services as defined in IDEA: an outcome-oriented process; based upon individual needs; including instruction, related services, community experiences, employment, and daily living and functional vocational evaluation.	
	When a student reaches age 14, IDEA requires the IEP team to consider post-school goals; and at age 16, an Individualized Transition Plan must be developed.	
Employment	A person who is competitively employed performs work valued by an employer, functions in an integrated setting with non-disabled co-workers, and earns at or above the minimum wage.	competitive employment
		supported employment
		mobile work crew
		enclave
	Supported Employment is competitive work in integrated settings for persons with severe disabilities, for whom competitive employment has not traditionally occurred, and who need intensive support services or extended services in order to perform such work.	natural supports
		self-management
		sheltered workshop

Chapter Fifteen at a Glance

Main Topics	Key Points	Key Terms
Employment (continued)	Four models of supported employment include small business enterprise, mobile work crew, enclave or workstation, and individual placement.	work activity center contracting prime manufacturing reclamation
	Sheltered employment is a vocational setting for adults with disabilities that offers transitional and extended employment. The problems with sheltered employment include limited opportunities for job placement and low pay.	
Postsecondary Education	Postsecondary education significantly improves chances of meaningful employment.	
	Increasingly jobs require technical training, problem-solving, and interpersonal skills that can be attained through postsecondary education.	
Residential Alternatives	Historically, segregation and institutionalization were the only options for persons with severe disabilities.	group homes foster homes apartment cluster co-residence apartment maximum independence apartment supported living deinstitutionalization
	Today most communities provide a variety of residential options including groups homes, foster homes, and various types of apartment living.	
	Supported living is the term used to describe a growing movement of helping people with disabilities live in the community as independently and normally as they possibly can.	
	Supported living is guided by individualization; future planning; use of connections; flexible supports; combining natural supports, learning, and technology; focusing on what people can do; using language that is natural to the setting; and ownership and control.	
	Deinstitutionalization, the movement of people with mental retardation out of large institutions and into small community-based living environments, has been an active reality for the past 30 years.	
Recreation and Leisure	Learning to participate in age-appropriate recreation and leisure activities is necessary for a self-satisfying life style.	
The Ultimate Goal: A Better Life	Adults with disabilities continue to face lack of acceptance as full members of society.	handicapism self-advocacy
	Handicapism, the discriminatory treatment and biased reactions toward someone with a disability, occurs on personal, professional, and societal levels.	
	Persons with disabilities have begun to assert their legal rights, challenging the view that persons with disabilities are incapable of speaking for themselves.	

Guided Review _____

I. How Do Former Special Education Students Fare as Adults?
    A. Completing High School

        • Only _____ of the students with disabilities exited high school with a diploma or certificate of completion in the 1999-2000 school year.
    B. Employment Status
        • The unemployment rate for young adults with disabilities is _____ when they have been out of school for 3-5 years.
    C. Postsecondary Education
        • _____ of young adults with disabilities are enrolled in postsecondary education programs within 3-5 years after leaving school compared with _____ of the general population.
    D. Overall Adjustment and Success
        • 37% live independently compared to 60% of the general population.
        • Four out of five former special education students had still not achieved the status of _____

        _____

II. Transition Services and Models
    A. Will's Bridges Model of School-to-Work Transition
        • Three levels of service: _____

        _____

    B. Halpern's Three-dimensional Model
        • Three domains: _____

        _____

    C. Definition of Transition Services in IDEA
        • outcome-oriented process; based upon individual needs; includes instruction, related services, community experiences, employment, and daily living and functional vocational evaluation

    D. Individualized Transition Plan
        • When a student reaches age 14, IDEA requires the IEP team to _____

        • When a student reaches age 16, _____

    E. Transition Teaming
        • Transition is a process involving the _____ of services from school to receiving agencies.

    F. Beginning Transition Activities and Career Education Early
        • Appropriate transition-related objectives should be selected at each age level, beginning in

        _____

III. Employment
    A. Competitive Employment
        • A person who is competitively employed _____

        _____

- Three characteristics of good secondary programs: _____

_____

B. Supported Employment
1. Supported employment is competitive work in integrated settings for persons with severe disabilities, for whom competitive employment has not traditionally occurred, and for whom intensive support services or extended services are needed in order to perform such work.

2. Small business enterprise: _____

_____

3. Mobile work crew: _____

_____

4. Enclave: _____

_____

4. Individual placement: _____

_____

- natural supports
- importance of co-workers
- natural cues and self-management

6. Sheltered employment:
- Sheltered workshops generally engage in one of three types of business ventures:

_____

- The problems with sheltered employment include: _____

_____

IV. Postsecondary Education
- Postsecondary education significantly improves the chances of _____

- Increasingly, jobs require _____

_____

- Even youth with moderate and severe disabilities can participate in some aspects of college life.

V. Residential Alternatives
- Historically, segregation and institutionalization were the only options for persons with severe disabilities.
- Today most communities provide a variety of _____

A. Group Homes
- provide family style living _____

- During the day, most residents _____

  B. Foster Homes
- As part of a family unit, the adult with disabilities also has more opportunities to interact with and be accepted by the community at large.

  C. Apartment Living
- offers a greater opportunity for integration into the community than group homes

- Three types of apartment living for adults with disabilities are: _____

_____

  D. Supported Living
- Supported living is the term used to describe _____

_____

- Supported living is guided by the following principles:
  individualization
  future planning

  use of _____

  flexible _____

  combining _____

  focusing on _____

  using language that is _____
  ownership and control

  E. Institutions
- inherent inability of institutional environment to _____

_____

- deinstitutationalization is _____

_____

VI. Recreation and Leisure
- Recreation and leisure activities do not come easily for many adults with disabilities.

- Too often leisure time of adults with disabilities is spent _____

- Special educators must realize the importance of _____

_____

VII. The Ultimate Goal: A Better Life
  A. Quality of Life
- Adults with disabilities continue to face lack of acceptance as full members of society.

  B. Misguided and Limiting Presumptions
- Handicapism, discriminatory treatment, and biased reactions toward someone with a disability occurs on personal, professional, and societal levels.

  C. Self-advocacy
- Persons with disabilities have begun to assert their legal rights, challenging the view that persons with disabilities are incapable of speaking for themselves.

  D. Still a Long Way to Go

In Class Activity

Small Group Activity: Develop transition skills curriculum for elementary school students

Transition planning for children with disabilities should really begin at the elementary school level. Identify a list of transition goals that would be appropriate for children with disabilities at the elementary school level.

Homework

Write a 2 page position paper on either of the following topics

1. Identify the most critical barriers to employment for adults with disabilities. Suggest strategies for overcoming the barriers to employment at the societal level and at the individual level.

2. Discuss the issues surrounding the right to get married and raise children for people with disabilities.

What Do You Think?
What are the most important indicators of quality of life for adults with disabilities?

According to your text, "Most advocates and professionals now realize that the physical presence of individuals with disabilities in integrated residential, work, and community settings is an important first step but that the only truly meaningful outcome of human service programs must be an improved quality of life." Write a 4-5 page paper explaining your conception and definition of "quality of life." Explain how quality of life can be measured within the context of your definition, and make recommendations of what must be done to improve the quality of life for adults with disabilities.

Resources and Suggestions for Exploration

Campo, S. F., & Sharpton, W. R. (1997). Correlates of the quality of life of adults with severe or profound mental retardation. Mental Retardation, 35, 329-338.

Green, C. W., Gardner, S. M., & Reid, D. H. (1997). Increasing indices of happiness among people with profound multiple disabilities: A program replication and component analysis. Journal of Applied Behavior Analysis, 30, 217-228.

Matikka, L. M., & Vesala, H. T. (1997). Acquiescence in quality-of-life interviews with adults who have mental retardation. Mental Retardation, 35, 75-79.

O'Brien, P., Thesing, A., Tuck, B., & Capie, A. (2001). Perceptions of change, advantage and quality of life for people with intellectual disability who left a long stay institution to live in the community. Journal of Intellectual and Developmental Disability, 26, 67-82.

Schalock, R. L. (2000). Three decades of quality of life. Focus on Autism and Other Developmental Disabilities, 15, 116-127.

Wehmeyer, M., & Schwartz, M. (1998). The relationship between self-determination and quality of life for adults with mental retardation. Education and Training in Mental Retardation and Developmental Disabilities, 33, 3-12.

Objectives

HOW DO FORMER SPECIAL EDUCATION STUDENTS FARE AS ADULTS?
1. List the outcome data for how former special educations students fare as adults.

TRANSITION MODELS AND SERVICES
1. Describe Will's Bridges Model of school-to-work transition.
2. Describe Halpern's three-dimensional model of transition.
3. List the components of an individualized transition plan.
4. Discuss the importance of collaboration and teaming.
5. Define and describe transition planning and when it should begin.

EMPLOYMENT
1. Describe the range of employment options for special education students.
2. Discuss the benefits and drawbacks of each employment option.

POSTSECONDARY EDUCATION
1. List the data for the number of special needs students attending postsecondary school.

RESIDENTIAL ALTERNATIVES
1. Describe the range of living arrangement alternatives available to adults with disabilities.

RECREATION AND LEISURE
1. Discuss the importance of teaching recreation and leisure skills.

THE ULTIMATE GOAL: A BETTER LIFE
1. List the areas that need improvement if students with special needs are to become more productive members of society.

Self-check Quiz

True/False

1. Sheltered workshops are considered an appropriate transition outcome for most students with disabilities.

2. An increasing self-advocacy is demonstrating that many persons with disabilities have the self-determination to speak for themselves.

3. The primary focus of transition planning is on establishment of postsecondary supports to foster success.

4. It is better to teach leisure and recreation skills that are commensurate to a person's mental age rather than their chronological age.

5. Career education for the disabled is a process begun at birth and continuing throughout life.

6. IDEA requires that transition planning begin when a student reaches the age of 14.

7. Co-worker involvement is important in supported employment, because co-workers can fix any errors the person with a disability may have made.

8. The primary characteristics of group homes that make them effective are small size and residential location.

9.   Institutions are generally considered an outdated and inappropriate residential option for individuals with disabilities.

10. Though only about 30% of students with disabilities complete high school, within 5 years about 25% complete a program to earn a diploma or GED.

11. Co-workers leaving their station to go on break is an example of a natural cue.

12. Reese is competitively employed by ProData, a company which pays him and other deaf students to write computer code for $20 an hour in an unsupervised setting.

13. IDEA requires transitional services for youth with disabilities.

14. The two primary criteria for having a high Quality of Life index are living in a community-based residence and working in an integrated setting.

15. The percentage of college students who indicate they have a disability has increased in recent years.

Essay Questions

1.   Compare and contrast models of supported employment; then highlight the ways in which they differ from competitive employment.

2.   For an individual with disabilities working in a grocery store, provide (a) three examples of natural cues, (b) an example of self-monitoring, and (c) an example of self-evaluation they might use.

Answers to Self-check Quiz Questions

Chapter 1
1. F; 2. F; 3. F; 4. T; 5. F; 6. T; 7. T; 8. F; 9. F; 10. T; 11. F; 12. T; 13. F; 14. T; 15. T

Chapter 2
1. F; 2. F; 3. T; 4. F; 5. T; 6. T; 7. T; 8. F; 9. T; 10. F; 11. T; 12. T; 13. F; 14. F; 15. T

Chapter 3
1. F; 2. F; 3. T; 4. F; 5. T; 6. F; 7. T; 8. T; 9. T; 10. F; 11. T; 12. F; 13. F; 14. F; 15. F

Chapter 4
1. T; 2. T; 3. T; 4. F; 5. T; 6. F; 7. F; 8. T; 9. F; 10. T; 11. T; 12. T; 13. F; 14. F; 15. T

Chapter 5
1. T; 2. F; 3. T; 4. F; 5. F; 6. F; 7. T; 8. F; 9. F; 10. F; 11. T; 12. F; 13. T; 14. F; 15. T

Chapter 6
1. T; 2. T; 3. F; 4. F; 5. T; 6. F; 7. T; 8. F; 9. T; 10. T; 11. F; 12. F; 13. F; 14. F; 15. T

Chapter 7
1. T; 2. T; 3. F; 4. T; 5. T; 6. F; 7. F; 8. T; 9. F; 10. F; 11. F; 12. T; 13. F; 14. T; 15. F

Chapter 8
1. F; 2. T; 3. T; 4. F; 5. T; 6. T; 7. F; 8. T; 9. F; 10. F; 11. F; 12. T; 13. F; 14. F; 15. T

Chapter 9
1. T; 2. T; 3. T; 4. T; 5. F; 6. T; 7. F; 8. F; 9. T; 10. F; 11. T; 12. T; 13. T; 14. F; 15. T

Chapter 10
1. T; 2. F; 3. F; 4. T; 5. F; 6. F; 7. T; 8. T; 9. F; 10. T; 11. F; 12. T; 13. F; 14. F; 15. T

Chapter 11
1. F; 2. T; 3. T; 4. T; 5. F; 6. F; 7. T; 8. F; 9. T; 10. T; 11. F; 12. F; 13. T; 14. T; 15. F

Chapter 12
1. F; 2. F; 3. T; 4. F; 5. T; 6. T; 7. F; 8. T; 9. F; 10. F; 11. T; 12. F; 13. T; 14. F; 15. F

Chapter 13
1. F; 2. F; 3. F; 4. T; 5. F; 6. T; 7. F; 8. T; 9. F; 10. T; 11. F; 12. T; 13. F; 14. F; 15. F

Chapter 14
1. F; 2. T; 3. T; 4. F; 5. F; 6. T; 7. F; 8. F; 9. T; 10. F; 11. T; 12. T; 13. F; 14. T; 15. F

Chapter 15
1. F; 2. T; 3. F; 4. F; 5. T; 6. T; 7. F; 8. T; 9. F; 10. F; 11. T; 12. F; 13. T; 14. F; 15. T